"Jeffrey Dean reminds us that the   s
changing just as fast as the technology. Parents need to read this book—
today."

—MIKE YORKEY, co-author of the Every Man's Battle series

"As our culture disengages more and more from Christian faith, it's
becoming harder and harder to follow Christ. This fact is hitting Christian teens very hard. Jeffrey Dean's book shows parents how to put on
their spiritual boxing gloves and fight for their children's destinies in
God. Read this very practical book!"

—BAYARD TAYLOR, author of *Blah, Blah, Blah: Making Sense
    of the World's Spiritual Chatter*

Praise for
This Is Me and *Watch This*

"*This Is Me* will encourage, inspire, and challenge anyone who dives in.
Many girls and women feel too scared or uncomfortable to talk about
these issues with a guy. For that reason this book possesses a uniqueness
that separates it from the pack. Not only is Jeffrey's approach on a very
personal level, it's packed with biblical truths. This book will change
your life if you're a young lady, a mother, or even a guy!"

—JOSH REEDY, lead singer, DecemberRadio

"Jeffrey Dean has a way of zeroing in on today's youth culture. He
knows teens and how to communicate the love of Jesus to them in a
way that captures their attention and convicts their hearts."

—JOSH D. MCDOWELL, author and communicator

"In *Watch This*, Jeffrey uses biblical truth to encourage teen guys to grow toward authentic manhood."

—JASON ROY, lead singer, Building 429

"Jeffrey Dean's *This Is Me* reads like an honest conversation with a trusted big brother. There are no catchy gimmicks or watered down lessons; just straight talk about the things girls care about most, backed up by Scripture, with all the authenticity that today's teens long for. I can't wait to share it with the girls in my life!"

—SHELLEY BREEN, singer with Point of Grace and author of *Life, Love, and Other Mysteries*

"In both *This Is Me* and *Watch This*, Jeffrey Dean has done a great job of identifying the things that matter most in life and conveying a message of hope for teens. His words are timeless and strong. You'll love what you read because it connects with the very heart of God."

—DANIEL S. WOLGEMUTH, president/CEO, Youth for Christ

"*This Is Me* is one of the most thorough, honest, biblical, and compassionate books I have read in quite some time. It's the kind of message I believe God will use to touch many teenagers across America. Jeffrey Dean is not only a talented musician and communicator, but God has given him a deep love for today's teenagers, and it shows. I highly recommend his work to you."

—DAWSON MCALLISTER, national talk-show host and youth communicator

"Among student communicators I've heard, I rate Jeffrey Dean among the top five. His message is relevant, clear, and biblical. He has a unique ability to relate to students about their culture and the choices they face. I highly recommend him."

—PHIL WALDREP, Phil Waldrep Ministries in Trinity, Alabama

THE FIGHT OF YOUR LIFE

Why your **teen**
is at risk &
what only **you**
can do about it

JEFFREY DEAN

MULTNOMAH
B O O K S

THE FIGHT OF YOUR LIFE
PUBLISHED BY MULTNOMAH BOOKS
12265 Oracle Boulevard, Suite 200
Colorado Springs, Colorado 80921

All Scripture quotations, unless otherwise indicated, are taken from the Holy Bible, New International Version®. NIV®. Copyright © 1973, 1978, 1984 by International Bible Society. Used by permission of Zondervan Publishing House. All rights reserved. Scripture quotations marked (HCSB) are taken from The Holman Christian Standard Bible®, © copyright 1999, 2000, 2002, 2003 by Holman Bible Publishers. Used by permission. Scripture quotations marked (MSG) are taken from The Message by Eugene H. Peterson. Copyright © 1993, 1994, 1995, 1996, 2000, 2001, 2002, 2005. Used by permission of NavPress Publishing Group. All rights reserved.

The stories contained in this book are true. Names and some details have been changed to protect privacy.

ISBN 978-1-60142-110-4
ISBN 978-1-60142-176-0 (electronic)

Published in the United States by WaterBrook Multnomah, an imprint of The Doubleday Publishing Group, a division of Random House Inc., New York.

MULTNOMAH and its mountain colophon are registered trademarks of Random House Inc.

Library of Congress Cataloging-in-Publication Data
Dean, Jeffrey
   The fight of your life : why your teen is at risk and what only you can do about it / by Jeffrey Dean. — 1st ed.
      p. cm.
   ISBN 978-1-60142-110-4
      1. Parenting—Religious aspects—Christianity. 2. Parent and teenager—Religious aspects—Christianity. 3. Christian teenagers—Religious life. 4. Christianity and culture. I. Title.
   BV4529.D425 2009
   248.8'45—dc22

                                                        2008039623

Printed in the United States of America
2009—First Edition

10 9 8 7 6 5 4 3 2 1

SPECIAL SALES
Most WaterBrook Multnomah books are available in special quantity discounts when purchased in bulk by corporations, organizations, and special-interest groups. Custom imprinting or excerpting can also be done to fit special needs. For information, please e-mail SpecialMarkets@WaterBrookMultnomah.com or call 1-800-603-7051.

—

For Amy…and all parents who are fighting
for our future world changers.

Contents

PART 3: HOPE AHEAD FOR EVERY FAMILY

DESPERATE TO KNOW HOW TO STAND FOR THE RIGHT

Dear Jeffrey,

Thanks so much for speaking at the festival last night. Your talk really helped bring me closer to God. I wish that my mom could've been there to hear what you said. I sort of have a hard time telling her the stuff that's really on my mind. When I do tell her stuff, she just says, "Well, that's how it is to be your age."

I just wish that someone somewhere would tell parents how hard it is to be a kid today. Whine, whine, whine, I know. But it's true—nobody ever tells them how hard it is to be a teenager. Like at school, everybody around me is all spiritual and stuff, but no one is really living for Christ. The kid next to me in trigonometry always brings his PDA to school and shows everybody dirty pictures when the teacher isn't looking. I doubt my teacher would even mind. She's a lesbian and always tells us all about her "summer with her lover."

Then there's Kaden. I met him in youth group, and he's really nice and all, but all of the girls he's ever dated have either gone all the way with him or at least had oral sex. I know he wants to do that with me because he's told me so. It's sort of embarrassing talking about this, but you've got to realize that in our school it's no big deal to hook up with someone, particularly if he says he's "into" you.

Jeffrey, what should I do? If I could just get my mom to know how hard this is, I know she could help me figure stuff out on an everyday basis. Even though we have our differences, my mom is pretty cool. The next time you talk to parents somewhere, please, please, please tell them what we have to fight against every day.

Sincerely,

Peyton

I wish I could say that Peyton's is an isolated story. But I hear from countless Christian teens just like Peyton across the country. The specifics of their stories are different, but inside these teens are searching for guidance. As parents who love God, we know it's important to guide the teens within our sphere of influence to real safety. I'm convinced that today's Christian teens are desperate to stand for what is right. But many aren't sure how to do so.

That's where you and I can help. It's a different world out there from when you and I were teens, and in the pages ahead we're going to do some battle training. The war is a fight for your teen's soul, and the consequences of losing can be deadly. But there is hope. Ephesians 6:10 encourages us to "be strong in the Lord and in his mighty power." The Bible gives us tools for suiting up in armor, taking up shields of faith, and holding firm the sword of the Spirit, the Word of God (see Ephesians 6:11–18). We're going to see how we can join the fight on behalf of the teens in our charge—not to render them helpless, but to strengthen them in their passage through the teen years.

Are you ready? My prayer is that you will be fearless along with me as we begin this fight together.

PART 1

THE FIGHT OF EVERY PARENT'S LIFE

A FIST FROM OUT OF NOWHERE

Grappling with the Enemy

Every teen is in a battle. Parent, did you know that? I'll say it again: every teen is in a battle. Including *your* teen.

If this "battle" talk sounds like a bit of a stretch to you, let me tell you about Rhys. A few summers ago I spoke at a camp. After an evening session, one of the guy counselors, Rhys, asked if we could talk. A clean-cut nineteen-year-old, Rhys was heading into his sophomore year at a well-known Christian college. His eyes reflected sadness that I couldn't fathom. He told me he had a lot of nightmares and a lot of guilt.

During his senior year of high school, Rhys and his girlfriend, Emily, were fairly typical Christian kids. They were both active in youth group, had pledged to abstain from sex until marriage, and were known in their circles of friends as "good kids."

But on the night of their senior prom, everything went crazy. Rhys admitted, "One thing led to another, and we pretty much did it all that night. Fooling around, drinking, drugs…you name it." Tragically, Emily overdosed on the drugs, went into a coma, and never came out of it. A week later, she died.

This is an extreme story, yes, but it happened. As I speak to high-school-age students around the country, I hear stories you wouldn't believe. Welcome to the world of today's teens. It's a fight, and every teen today is engaged in it.

This fight is about a tsunami of information, communication, anything-goes ethics, and the inevitable moral experimentation that results. It's a world of light-speed Internet, texting, unlimited access to online porn, oral-sex parties, MySpace, cutting, Wicca, drinking, drugs, and more.

The world of today's teens moves at a pace you and I would never have dreamed of when we were teens. It's a world where *hooking up* has nothing to do with a fishing lure, *spam* isn't something you eat, and *pharming* doesn't require a tractor. Almost weekly, teens write to me about addictions to types of drugs that weren't around twenty years ago. At seminars across the country, I meet students who have contracted sexually transmitted diseases.

By the time they graduate from high school, most seniors tell me, they have consumed alcohol and been offered drugs. Most teens I meet say that marijuana is easily accessible. It doesn't matter whether they attend public schools or Christian schools; students know where drugs are used, kept, and sold. Many tell me they know a friend or classmate who has abused prescription drugs.

Here's the fact that keeps me awake at night: Rhys and Emily could have been anyone's teens. They are from a generation of teens bombarded by lies, hungry for help, and desperate for truth. Not every teen will face exactly what Rhys and Emily faced, but war is the daily reality for every teen.

That is why I say that as a parent, you are facing the fight of your life.

Why This Book Is for Every Parent

Maybe you're thinking this book isn't for you. Your teen appears to be doing well. And it's true: there are many Bible-believing, church-attending teens who desire to live lives surrendered to Christ. Your teen may be one of them.

Or maybe you're at the other end of the spectrum. The choices your teen has made so far have pushed your family to the breaking point. You're feeling hopeless, ready to throw in the towel.

Wherever your teen is at in his or her journey, this book is for you. No matter what the situation looks like on the surface, every teen faces struggles, temptations, issues, fears, and challenges. Every teen has to navigate the confusing waters of today's culture. Every teen is only one choice away from hurt, addiction, heartbreak, and more.

The scary thing with teenagers is that often we don't know exactly what they're thinking or feeling, even when they live under our own roofs! For the past fifteen years, I've been touring the country, speaking—and more important, *listening*—to teens. Some three hundred fifty thousand teens a year check out my Web site, and more than fifty thousand read and respond to my blog. Teens tell me things they often don't share with their parents. That's why I wanted to write this book—not to break their confidences, but to give you the inside scoop on what I'm hearing so you can help your teen in the battle.

In the struggles teens face, they have a common enemy: the devil. And he hates these kids. More specifically, he's *your* teen's number one enemy. His task is to steal, kill, and destroy (see John 10:10), and he wants to lure your teen away from the truth and lead your teen toward destruction. Sure, movement toward destruction is more evident in some teens than in others. But no teen is immune to spiritual warfare.

So, as a parent, your call is to grab your weapons, jump into the battle-field on your teen's side, and be ready to give it all you've got.

Playing Offense

The idea of *fighting* for your teen might almost scare you off. Hey, you're just trying to pay the electric bill, pick up the kids from soccer practice on time, and serve something for dinner that didn't come from a drive-through.

But I won't sugarcoat what's happening in your teen's world. As a parent, you are engaged in one of the greatest fights of your life. It's already on, whether you want it or not. Every day a war is being waged for the soul of your teen. The question isn't, are you at war? The question is, are you equipped to do battle?

Here's what the Bible says about it: "Pursue righteousness, godli-ness, faith, love, endurance and gentleness. *Fight the good fight of the faith*" (1 Timothy 6:11–12, emphasis added).

"Fight the good fight"—that's the battle you are in. You are called to faithfully fight for what's right. Just as Satan is fighting to steal, kill, and destroy your teen, so you must be a fighter, helping your teen to win!

Recently a mother talked to me about her teenage son. "Jeffrey," she said, "my son has never smoked pot, checked out porn, or been sex-ually active. His grades are good, and his friends are well behaved. He loves going to youth group at church and believes God is calling him into pastoral ministry. I am so glad that God has given us our son."

I congratulated her on the successes of her son and on her parent-ing skills, then asked, "What are you doing each day to ensure that your son continues down this good road?"

"What do you mean?" she said, looking perplexed.

"What steps have you put into place to safeguard your son from the Enemy?"

"I don't know," she said, "Everything's going so well—I haven't thought about it much."

Together we discussed a plan for her to pray daily for her son, to keep speaking truths into his life, and to keep the lines of communication open with him about his personal life. Most important, we talked about ways she could continue to help him grow in a daily and intimate walk with God.

That's what the fight looks like in action.

It's easy to believe that good parenting means checking off a list of positive accomplishments for a son or daughter:

√ My teen is a Christian.

√ My teen regularly attends youth group.

√ My teen dates a Christian (or doesn't date at all).

√ My teen doesn't watch MTV.

√ My teen _____ (has this form of observable good behavior).

You may be able to place a check beside any one or all of these statements. But helping your teen through these intense years isn't simply about completing a checklist. You need to be looking ahead, adapting and strategizing as the flow of the battle changes, and working to guide your teen through obstacles to victory. It means approaching parenting on the offense as you work toward a goal, rather than sitting back and waiting for the other side to come at you.

Undoubtedly you've heard messages about how to deal with personal struggles, how to climb back up after failing, how to overcome addictions, and the like. But what if, rather than living life on cruise control, you lived life on enemy patrol—watching, being prepared, planning, developing a game plan for life, and putting into practice the principles that shape character and truth?

This is the idea behind the warning God gives in 1 Peter 5:8: "Be self-controlled and alert. Your enemy the devil prowls around like a roaring lion looking for someone to devour."

God has not created you to simply survive. He has created you to thrive, to experience the abundant life. When it comes to your teen, 1 Peter 5:8 warns that parents must be found with weapon in hand, ready to fight on behalf of their teens.

A mom recently said to me, "I realized years ago that I can't sit around assuming that my kids are going to naturally come talk to me about all the stuff in their lives. I have to go to them. I have to initiate conversations. I have to look for moments of opportunity to get them talking. Because if I don't, I'll probably never know what they're up against out there."

That's it! This mother is in the war room every day, plotting against the Enemy of her teen. She's studying the Enemy's tactics so she can guard her teen as he moves toward a deeper and more intimate walk with God.

The Confidence to Go for It

The idea of fighting can seem daunting. But my goal in this book isn't to scare you. It's to help you see that the fight is real, that you're in it whether you like it or not, and that you can win the war.

This is your moment. When God created you, He created you to be the parent your teen needs you to be. God would never have given you the privilege of being a parent if He didn't have an awesome plan for you in the process. God has called you to be a fighter—and He has given you everything you need to fight and to win for your teen.

This book will help you go the distance. In the pages ahead, we'll discuss strategies for going on the offense. We'll talk about what it means to study your teen's culture so you can live with your eyes wide open—ready, armed, and alert. We'll talk about how one of your greatest strategies, prayer, is actually one of the simplest, and how the prayer of a righteous parent is an incredibly powerful and effective tool in this fight (see James 5:16). We'll talk about specific issues your teen is facing (issues that definitely were not around when you were a teen), and we'll look at how these issues don't need to surprise you or catch you off guard. We'll look at specific, detailed battle plans that include the tools and resources you need. We'll talk about how your role isn't to prop up your teen or ultimately save him or her, but to teach discernment and provide a solid foundation from which your teen can do battle. We'll show you how to provide your teen with armor for fighting and wings for flying. And we'll talk about the incredible privilege you have been given to encourage your teen to live wholeheartedly for our Lord and Savior Jesus Christ, the fighter who is greater than anything this world can throw your teen's way.

Your Fighting Positions

Right from the get-go, let's take a look at five main fighting positions necessary for being armed and active in this fight. Keep these fighting positions in mind as you move forward to the following chapters.

The Sweeping Aside Motion

This means, the past is in the past. Helping your teen win the war isn't about questioning what you could have done yesterday. It is about establishing a battle plan for what you are going to do today, tomorrow, and beyond. It's never too late to reach out to your teen, to learn to communicate again, to listen, to speak words of wisdom into your teen's life. Start today.

The Gritting Your Teeth Gesture

This means, whatever it takes is whatever it takes. There will be times when you will be challenged to move out of your comfort zone. Your goal must be to arm yourself for battle and be ready to do whatever is necessary to help your teen through these entangling years. Be fearless.

The Ultimate Power Stance

This means, pray for your teen every day. The Ultimate Power Stance is kneeling. If you are not praying for your teen every day, start now. If you are, keep it up. Prayer is the key to it all. I can't reiterate this enough. Praying for your teen is the single most powerful tool you have in this fight.

The Open Book Motion

This means, you are now a student of teen culture. The world moves at an incredibly fast pace today. To keep up with what's up in your teen's world takes time, energy, effort, and motivation. What's current today might not have been current yesterday. From here on out, make it one of your primary ambitions to study and learn about the world your teen lives in.

The Deep Breath Posture

This means, the battle is a fight of endurance. You develop a realistic strategy for success by taking it one step at a time. Remember, winning the fight is not about doing everything today. It's about being faithful over the long haul.

Power for Your Toughest Job

Parenting is likely the toughest job you will ever have. Don't assume that your teen is exempt from any issue discussed in the coming pages. At some point, on some level, every teen will encounter every issue described in this book. As a parent, you need to be equipped. It is my hope that this book will be a powerful resource you use to arm yourself and your teen to win the battle being waged for his or her soul.

Remember the Ultimate Power Stance? Let's take a moment to pray right now for your teen, for what we'll talk about ahead in this book, and for how life may change.

Praying Scripture for Your Teen

Lord, You say in Your Word that if we seek You we'll be able to find You. Troubles may come and awful things may happen, but You listen and You care. You're a compassionate God. You will not abandon my family. Please guide me in this fight for my teen. You are God. You are good. Give me Your strength, Your wisdom, and Your perspective. I put my trust in You. Amen.

BASED ON DEUTERONOMY 4:29

2

REALITY IS HARD TO HEAR

But It's Important to Know
What's Happening

The coolest person in my dorm at Belmont University was a guy named Blake. I hate to say it, but it was all because of what he owned. It was something extremely rare for a college student twenty years ago.

It was a personal computer.

Laughable, huh?

Today's teens are more electronic than ever before. How many of the following is your teen familiar with? A desktop, laptop, cell phone, iPod, PDA, BlackBerry Pearl, RAZR, Sidekick 3, UTStarcom Slice, MP3 player, MP4 player, DVD player, HD DVD player, Blu-ray player... As soon as you blink, there's something else added to the list.

I'm not against gaming, surfing, downloading, blogging, listening to music, watching videos, or chatting on social-networking sites. But an overall escalating trend can cause problems: a barrage of messages and images is being downloaded into your teen's heart and head daily.

Some of these messages are informative, entertaining, and positive. But some of them can be harmful. Very harmful.

Let me make something clear: the culture around us is not the enemy. Satan is. But Satan and his cohorts use the culture in persuasive ways. And like it or not, media, entertainment, and communication tools are here to stay.

How the World Has Changed

Your teen lives in a different world than you did when you were a teen. Today's global connectedness is only one example of how the world has shifted. There have even been changes in basic ideas about reality.

Each generation takes steps to experiment, challenge, and wrestle with such issues as truth, God, and morality. And in that respect, today's generation is no different. But I want to point out five key trends of today's culture that make up a world that may not be guided by the logic you are familiar with. As you consider these new paradigms of thought and belief, don't forget the Open Book Motion—you need to be a student of teen culture.

Right and Wrong? Well, It Depends

Teens today have been told countless times through popular culture that right and wrong are personal decisions, not absolutes. They've been assured that morals and ethics are not dictated by God; they're dictated by personal choice. In this faulty belief system, it's considered okay to do anything you want any way you want to, as long as it works for you in the moment. For instance, choosing the homosexual lifestyle isn't morally wrong; it's just another way of living.

I find this harmful belief system permeating the lives of both Christian and non-Christian teens. For instance, at a recent conference I explained at length the ideas mentioned above, then asked, "Just out of curiosity, how many of you believe there is absolute truth?"

In an audience of more than twelve hundred teens, only about one hundred raised their hands.

Does that shock you? It means that only about 10 percent of today's teens believe that things can be absolutely considered right or wrong. When it comes to morality and ethics, the other 90 percent just go with their guts.

How might this trend emerge in the life of your teen or your teen's friends? Without biblically grounded concepts of right and wrong, today's teens have been shown to be more likely to:

- cheat on an exam
- lie to a friend (or a parent)
- steal from a store or off the Internet (such as downloading a song without paying for it)
- physically hurt someone
- attempt suicide[1]

Recently I was talking with a senior citizen in my church. He told me that even though he hadn't been raised as a Christian, he and all his friends were quite moral when they were teens. If someone lost his or her virginity before marriage, it was scandalous. If a teen showed up at a party drunk, he was considered a troublemaker. If a kid was known to cheat on a test at school, other kids watched that person with a wary eye.

---

1. Josh McDowell with Bob Hostetler, "Today's Youth Need Our Help to Go...Beyond Belief," *Enrichment Journal,* Fall 2006, http://enrichmentjournal .ag.org/200604/200604_036_BeyondBelief.cfm (accessed June 13, 2008).

Sixty years ago there were prescribed social norms of morality. Today the trend is relativism. It's a dangerous belief system that means whatever goes is whatever goes.

The New Cool? You'll Never Guess

Twenty years ago, when I was in high school, it was an insult to call another guy a homosexual. Now, I'm not suggesting that today's culture should go back to the place where it was considered cool to insult people living a homosexual lifestyle. But I want to point out that today the trend has reversed.

Recently I received this e-mail from a teen who attends a church I spoke at: "I date both guys and girls," wrote Parker, fifteen. "I don't think there is anything wrong with it. I'm a Christian, and I know God says that we should love everyone. So dating both sexes is my way of doing just that."

This trend may sound shocking, but it's actually cool today for a teen to be considered "queer" (the new popular word for homosexuality). A Web site for teens declares, "Being gay can be fun and exciting, with lots of opportunities to help out and acquire a reputation as a really cool person. Here's how!"[2]

How did homosexuality make this transition?

While it was once a taboo topic, homosexuality is now celebrated in mainstream media. Television sitcoms and reality shows are leading a not-so-quiet revolution that's flooded with innuendos and messages promoting same-sex marriages and bisexuality. Private schools are springing up across the country luring teens who are often insecure and

---

2. Scott Bidstrup, "The Cool Page for Queer Teens," Veritas Et Ratio—Truth and Reason, www.bidstrup.com/cool.htm (accessed June 13, 2008).

confused into what they call a "get centered" environment that promotes homosexuality as the new normal. Shelters across the nation advertise on high-traffic Web sites for what are known as LGBT centers—lesbian, gay, bisexual, and transgender homes for teens.

The homosexual revolution has worked. Homosexuality has made the leap from being avoided to being the new cool.

Sex Ed Isn't What It Seems

Several years ago I was approached by a parent who heard that I would be speaking at her daughter's school the following day. This mother of three assured me that it was not necessary for me to speak about abstinence in her daughter's school because abstinence was already being taught to the students in health class. This well-meaning mother thought it would be a better use of my time to speak to the students about another topic.

What she did not realize was that even though the state in which she lived had a law requiring the public schools to teach abstinence, this school also chose to teach that abortion is an option for teens who choose to be sexually active.

Just because your state law requires that your teen be taught abstinence does not mean that a health teacher or principal will not choose to also teach other options when it comes to sex. At first glance, abstinence-based sex education sounds good, but often it is not. Abstinence-based sex ed rarely teaches that abstinence is the healthiest lifestyle choice. Instead, it usually presents abstinence (defined as avoiding sexual intercourse) as *one option* for teens while at the same time promoting other sexual practices.

For example, in one city in which I recently spoke, the public junior high school was using the abstinence-based sex-ed approach.

School district officials contracted me for a day to cover the abstinence part of their six-week sex-ed class for eighth graders. The week previous, another speaker had been brought into the school to cover "how to use a condom the right way." Students were given cucumbers to practice applying condoms. Students were also introduced to various kinds of body gels, lubricants, oils, and lotions for use during mutual masturbation.

Another abstinence-based sex-ed program provided a time during class for teens to be creative in thinking of ways to be "close" to their dates, such as showering together, checking out porn together, looking at erotic magazines or books, and engaging in mutual masturbation.

Unfortunately, this is the reality of what many teens are learning in school, even in those school districts that profess to operate under an abstinence-only curriculum.

Spirituality Is In

Our culture has never been more "spiritual" than it is today. But the problem is that while many teens believe in God, their beliefs about Him are defined by the culture, not by the Bible. A recent survey of American teens showed that although the majority of the teens surveyed claimed some form of Christianity as their religion, few could describe the tenets of their religion and what it means.[3]

So where do today's teens get their ideas about God? Well, certainly from their parents. But certainly also from popular cultural leaders such as Oprah and her New Age guru Eckhart Tolle, who espouses a blend of Eastern and Western mysticism.

---

3. Christian Smith, National Study of Youth and Religion, quoted in "Understanding the Religious and Spiritual Lives of Teenagers," Saint George Greek Orthodox Church, 2005, www.stgeorgegoc.org/PastorsCornerTeenSpirituality.html (accessed June 14, 2008).

Widespread spiritual teaching always filters down to teens. Be wary of cultural leaders who may mention and even promote Jesus Christ but who also strongly promote words and concepts such as these:

- spirit
- new earth
- spiritual awakenings
- God concept (or Christ concept)
- Christ consciousness or higher consciousness

Of course, such words and concepts may be used within the Christian community as well. But usage of these terms by your teen should be cause for you to carefully examine his or her intentions.

At a recent conference, I outlined some of the core beliefs of Christianity, then asked a group of teens to write what the bottom line was with them and their faith. That is, if their faith could be boiled down to one sentence, what would it be? Here are snippets from some of their responses:

I believe all religions lead to the same God. (Anna, fourteen)

There's more than one way to heaven. (Carter, fifteen)

Sure, Jesus sinned. Everybody sins. (Zoe, sixteen)

Hell isn't real. I think hell is just in your mind. (Gabrielle, fifteen)

Of course, I believe in evolution—doesn't everybody with a brain? (Jordan, seventeen)

What's most important is that you treat other people with tolerance. (Evan, sixteen)

Christianity, Hinduism, Islam, Judaism—everybody prays to the same God. It's just that God has different ways he (or she) is seen. (Bailey, eighteen)

What's really cool is spiritual power. My friend is into Wicca, and she's told me some things that you absolutely wouldn't believe could happen. (Paige, fourteen)

That last student's comment brings me to the next trend I see.

The Dark Side Has More Fans

Have you heard of words such as *magik, coven, esbat, sabbat,* or *druidism?* Your teen probably has.

Such words may look and sound like words from the latest sci-fi movie. But actually these words are associated with the modern neo-pagan movement known as Wicca. In the past few years, the Wiccan movement has leaped in popularity. It used to have a minimal following. Now it's a religion with mainstream interest. Today Wicca is considered cool to many teens and young adults.

Wicca basically means "the craft of the wise," but actually, Wicca is a modern form of witchcraft. Why has it become so popular? Just ask a few teens what TV shows they've watched or books they've read in recent years. This is what you'll hear: *Charmed, Buffy the Vampire Slayer,* and *Sabrina, the Teenage Witch* as well as the Harry Potter series. These products have whetted the appetites of today's teens for the mysteriousness of the supernatural.

A Wiccan follower abides by a creed called "the Rede," which states, "And harm ye none, do what ye will." Basically this means that as long as what you are doing does not hurt anyone, you can do whatever you want. With its lack of rules, Wicca has become an appealing religion to a generation of teens with little belief in absolutes. An extremely popular attraction of Wicca is its anything-goes sexual mentality. Homosexuality, premarital sex, oral sex, bisexuality, and nudity are all normal and accepted practices under the Wiccan Rede.

On the surface, Wicca looks safe to many teens. I have found that many teens turn to Wicca initially because they feel accepted by the Wiccan community. Many of these teens, in their search for significance, are vulnerable and willing to plug in to something different, even if they do not fully understand the extent of the possible spiritual oppression that comes with Wicca.

The obvious concern, if your teen is experimenting with Wicca, is that it is not in line with God's Word. No matter how appealing Wicca looks, nothing that is out of God's will is ever okay. Wicca takes the focus of one's life, purpose, and destiny off God and places it onto nature and self-serving practices.

Some Good News

After reading through those trends, you may be feeling burdened and concerned about the state of today's teens, the future of our nation, and how your teen fits into all of this. Your concern can be a powerful tool as you assume a greater understanding of the war being waged for the soul of your teen.

I find great comfort in Jeremiah 29:11: "'I know the plans I have for you,' declares the LORD, 'plans to prosper you and not to harm you, plans to give you hope and a future.'" What a great promise from God in this verse! No matter how maddening the world is, God's message is timeless. God is still in control. And He still wants to bless your teen with an abundant life.

What is the key to inheriting this promise? The answer is found in the next two verses of Jeremiah 29: "Then you will call upon me and come and pray to me, and I will listen to you. You will seek me and find me when you seek me with all your heart." Teens find hope when they choose to seek God with *all* their hearts.

Satan clearly understands this. If the Enemy can keep a teen away from pursuing a committed relationship with Jesus Christ throughout the teen years, then he has likely gained a soul for life. You need to be aware of the reality of the cultural war that the evil spirits are waging against your teen. Satan knows the good plans God has for your teen, and Satan wants to release all hell on earth to keep your teen from becoming everything that God promises he or she can be.

But don't lose heart. I've saved the best news for last: although Satan is out to end it all for our teens, we have Someone on our side who is greater than he who is in the world (see 1 John 4:4). Look at what Jesus says He has for us, and our teens, in John 10:10: "I have come that they may have life, and have it to the full."

If you can help your teen to have a correct understanding of God, based on His Word, then you will be empowering your teen to understand the errors of this culture. As you continue to read, it is my hope that you will become more encouraged, more determined, and more equipped with the information and resources you need to empower your teen to fight the good fight and ultimately receive the abundant life Jesus promises.

Let's close this chapter with the Ultimate Power Stance.

Praying Scripture for Your Teen

God, You say in Your Word that You are always with us, and if we will seek You, we will find You. Thank You that You lovingly look after all those who seek You. Let me be this type of parent, and help me guide my teen toward the abundant life You offer. Amen.

BASED ON 2 CHRONICLES 15:2 AND EZRA 8:22

3

DREAMING BIG FOR YOUR TEEN

Keep the Goal in Mind

I will never forget the night our first child, Bailey Faith, was born. Words cannot describe the overwhelming joy I felt as I stood in the delivery room holding our baby girl for the first time. After a special time alone as a family, we let our daughter be taken to the hospital nursery for her first nap outside the womb. My wife, Amy, slipped off to sleep. But I couldn't—I was wired with new-daddy excitement! I walked the hall to the nursery, where, gazing through the window with tear-filled eyes, I watched my daughter sleep for the first time.

As I stood there, thoughts raced through my mind. I wanted to hold my little girl again, to take her in my arms, never let go of her, and forever protect her from the outside world. I had visions of being Super Dad—never messing up, always being there for her, doing everything within my power to ensure she had the perfect life. I imagined how it would be to watch her grow, crawl, and walk and how one day she would speak her first word (which, of course, would be "Daddy"!). I smiled as I thought of her growing up, riding a bike, going to school, making friends, having parties, and eventually starting to date (when she turned twenty-seven). I took a deep breath and said, "I'm a dad. How cool is this! We are going to have so much fun!"

Do you remember a similar scene when your first child was born? Remember those little hands and feet and that cute nose? Remember how you couldn't take your eyes off your child? Remember how you were consumed with love? Remember the hopes and dreams you had for your baby? It's no wonder God describes Himself throughout Scripture as a parent. For instance, in Isaiah 9:6 He says He is our "Everlasting Father." There's no more unconditional love on earth than that of parents for their own child. The love we feel for our children can be intoxicating.

And now your baby is a teenager. A lot has changed since those first days of your child's life, hasn't it? One minute your child relied on you

KNOW THY TEEN

Here is a practical way to regain a dream for your teen if you are no longer dreaming big. Think about who your teen truly is. What's the overall state of your teen's life?

You may want to grab a pen and paper right now and think through this list:

1. My teen's greatest strengths are...
2. My teen's greatest struggles are...
3. The thing I love most about my teen is...
4. My teen's closest friends are...
5. My teen's walk with God is characterized by...

for everything. Then you blinked. Pacifiers, bottles, blankets, and teddy bears have been replaced with cell phones, iPods, laptops, and Game Boys. You and your child are facing a new world of challenges and influences. The idea of leading your teen through the entangling adolescent years can seem overwhelming. But you can do this.

And part of the strategy is to keep dreaming.

Dreaming Big

In a book about being a fighter for your teen, it's easy to lose sight of dreaming big for your teen. By "dreaming big," I mean praying that the teen in your care will experience a life blessed with happiness, success, and God's richest favor. You dream that your teen will become all God wants him or her to be.

6. My teen spends his or her free time by...
7. If I were to read the last hundred text messages or e-mails my teen has sent, I would probably learn that...

Part of the intention in the above exercise is to help you see areas in your teen's life where you will need to fight alongside your teen. Maybe you recognize a pattern that is slowly eroding your teen's character and leading your teen to embrace a lifestyle contrary to God's will. Hopefully you also see strengths and gifts that God has given to your teen, so that you can continually encourage your teen to grow as he or she fights the good fight.

Do you still dream of the best for your teen? It can be easy to stop doing so. In the hustle and flow of a busy life, little by little a dream is replaced by reality. The hope for a better tomorrow is replaced by a hope to just get through each day. But look at what this verse says about dreams and hopes for your teen:

> Why are you downcast, O my soul?
>> Why so disturbed within me?
>> Put your hope in God. (Psalm 42:11)

Your teen needs you to keep dreaming for him or her. Your teen needs you to *put your hope in God* and take God at His word.

If you've lost hope for your teen's future or for your ability to guide him or her, remember, God is able to work miracles in your life and the life of your teen. Even if your teen appears to be doing well, keep hoping. God has much more to do in your teen's life.

I am not saying that you should push your teen to only live out *your* dreams. I'm saying that you want the best for your teen's life. You want *God's* dream for your teen to come true. That's the dream to keep alive.

Truth and Lies

Your teen is growing up in a world that constantly says your teen isn't rich enough, good looking enough, skinny enough (or muscular enough), smart enough, sexy enough, athletic enough, popular enough, or capable enough. As parents, it is sometimes possible to ingest these messages and start believing them ourselves, particularly when a relationship with a teen is strained.

But God's Word says otherwise. I am convinced that many teens haven't fully reached their potential because they have never had someone fully explain to them how God sees them. They have allowed Satan or the culture or a friend or a sibling or the mirror or a magazine or a movie or a coach or a teacher or perhaps even a parent to sell them a lie. Have you ever caught yourself saying things like this to your teen?

- "You will never be as good as your brother."
- "Look how pretty she is. You'll never look like that."
- "You've blown it now. You'll never amount to anything."
- "God could never forgive that."
- "You're so stupid. Why don't you just give up?"

If so, the point is not to berate yourself. Remember the Sweeping Aside Motion, one of the fighting positions we talked about in chapter 1. It means the past is in the past. Helping your teen win the war isn't about questioning what you could have done yesterday. It is about establishing a game plan for what you are going to do today, tomorrow, and beyond.

Probably each of us at one time or another has heard and believed such lies as the bulleted statements above. This is why it's important to know how God sees people. It's vital for your teen to understand who he or she really is in Christ. And it's important for you to know these truths as well. Why? Because as you begin to see your teen as God does, you will be better able to communicate these truths to your teen. This is important because your teen will live as he or she believes.

A Heavenly Perspective on Your Teen

Let's take a look at several principles based on Scripture that show how God sees your teen. These principles are key in developing a new dream for your teen.

Your Teen Reflects God's Glory

Your teen has been created in the image of God (see Genesis 1:27). This is the foundation of all true self-worth.

After counseling thousands of teens, I have found one common denominator: many teens do not like themselves. Countless voices constantly tell teens they don't measure up. But your teen needs to hear from you—often—something like this: "You may not like who you are. You may not feel valuable. But God believes your value is immeasurable. That's why He created you."

Being created to reflect God's character means that your teen is capable of honoring God in every area of life, including handling pressure, dealing with sex and dating, saying no to drugs and alcohol, and maintaining integrity when no one's looking.

How might this truth exhibit itself in a family setting?

I was speaking at a conference last summer when a girl approached me after the event and asked if we could talk. Callie, fourteen, said she was struggling with self-confidence. Anytime a teacher called on her in class, her face turned red. She didn't have many friends. She felt awkward and stupid around her peers, even though she excelled on the school's debate team and made the principal's list every semester.

Callie and I talked about this very principle—that she was created in the image of God and reflected His glory. I took her to Genesis 1:27 and showed her what God thinks of her. We talked about how Callie could imagine God walking the hallways of her school alongside her. Anytime she didn't feel like she measured up, she could imagine God whispering in her ear, "Callie, I think the world of you." When Callie left, she was smiling.

Now, I'm not so naive as to believe that Callie will never struggle with issues of self-worth again. Change is usually a process. But she now has a foundation of truth to build on. What will really help is if her parents reinforce this truth.

Your Teen Has Been Given Responsibility

God created Adam and Eve to live in the Garden of Eden, and life in the garden must have been amazing. Adam and Eve had everything they could ever want: a place to live, no rent, no bills, food, a beautiful backyard, each other. And since clothes weren't even invented yet, they didn't have to worry about getting dressed—ever.

Adam and Eve did have responsibilities, though. At Creation God outlined one important role that Adam and Eve—and every human since them—were called to fulfill. God said, "I'm giving you the privilege of being responsible for all of my creation. Don't blow it; don't abuse it. Use this privilege wisely" (see Genesis 1:26–30).

Does your teen know this? If we could watch a sixty-minute DVD summarizing the previous year of your teen's life, what would we see? We know that he or she has been created as a person of responsibility, not to just do whatever he or she wants, but to use abilities, gifts, and individuality wisely. Yet your teen may not be living that way.

Colton, thirteen, asked to talk with me after a session at a youth retreat a few months ago. His number one problem in life? He "felt bored all the time" because there was "never anything to do." I asked him how he typically spent his free time. "I dunno. Just hanging out playing video games," he said.

Colton needed a task. I took him to Genesis 2:19–20 and talked about how he had a fundamental need inside him to do something important. He was created for a purpose. God designed Colton to be responsible. Together we brainstormed things he might do to find and fulfill his purpose.

It turns out that Colton had always loved dogs, and he had thought about volunteering to train guide dogs for the blind. Colton just didn't know how to start or even that he was capable of doing some really cool things. We talked about how he might talk to his parents when he got home and about how he could research companies that specialize in guide-dog training and see what the next step could be.

Your Teen Has Been Marvelously Made

It can be tough for your teen to know that he or she has been marvelously created (see Psalm 139:14). Read what one teen girl recently told me: "Um…excuse me. He didn't make a mistake? You've got to be kidding. I'm a walking mistake, with all my fat and zits and my ugly hair and big nose."

It is important that you be armed and ready to combat the pain and hurt your teen is struggling with. Knowing that God carefully created your teen doesn't change the fact that your daughter may have pimples or your son may have a nose he doesn't care for. And just because you convey this truth to her or him doesn't mean that tomorrow your teen will wake up, look in the mirror, and love what's there.

For your teen to see himself or herself through God's eyes is a tough challenge. Your teen's eyes have been trained by the world to see all his or her physical flaws—and nothing else. Your teen's ability to see himself or herself as God intended is about learning to look beyond the things your teen doesn't like. It's about realizing he or she has been created exactly the way God wanted.

To God, your teen is unique. He has an amazing plan for your teen's life that may require zits and a big nose to make it complete. Your teen might not be able to see the plan yet, but God has a reason behind every "flaw" and a purpose behind every imperfection.

The demonic forces are fighting to convince your teen that who he or she sees in the mirror will never be enough. You must fight to help your teen see otherwise. Your teen has been created by God.

How to Keep Dreaming for Your Teen

When God created your teen, He didn't make a mistake. So keep dreaming the dream for your teen. As you do, help your teen to see this dream. The goal is for your teen to realize that God created him or her exactly as intended, that he or she has a purpose, and that God has a plan for each person. God wants each person to live abundantly, with all the blessings He provides.

How might you apply the principles expressed in this chapter?

It's important to ingest the scriptural principles yourself first. Do you really know that your teen was created in the image of God, that your teen was designed to be responsible, and that your teen has been marvelously made? You may want to spend some time meditating on the Scripture verses cited for each principle above.

It's also important to spend time talking with your teen. Where does your teen like to hang out? Take him or her out for a burger or soda, a ball game, a concert, a trip to the park. Ask yourself where your teen is most open to conversation. Then start a conversation by asking questions and listening to your teen's answers. Ask open-ended questions such as these:

- "What's been going on in your life lately?"
- "How are things with your friends?"
- "How have things been going for you at school lately?"

Gradually, get to the point in your conversation where you can bring up what you want to discuss. Ask your teen what his or her main struggles are right now. Or what his or her main joys are.

It might feel strange at first to show your teen a Bible verse that applies to his or her life, particularly if you've never done something like that before. But this is where at least three of the main fighting positions we talked about in the first chapter factor in. You may have to use the Gritting Your Teeth Gesture, meaning that whatever it takes is whatever it takes. Be bold, be sensitive, and have the courage to initiate deep conversations with your teen. Then apply the Ultimate Power Stance to your conversation. Pray like mad (silently is okay) that God would show you what to say and what not to say. And the Deep Breath Posture fits here as well. You may not be able to say all you want to say in one conversation with your teen. That's okay; there will be more conversations to come. Remember, winning the fight is not about doing everything today. It's about being faithful over the long haul. This is a fight of endurance.

You can do it. You can dream new dreams for your teen. God will help. Let's do some praying for this right now.

Praying Scripture for Your Teen

God, thank You that my teen was marvelously made. I worship You in adoration—You know what You're doing. God, You know my teen inside and out; You know every bone in my teen's body. You know exactly how my teen was made, bit by bit. Give me the strength, grace, and courage I need to instill these scriptural principles in my teen's life. Lord, all of my teen's days are spread before You like an open book. All the stages of my teen's life were prepared before my teen had even lived one day. Help me, Lord, to guide my teen in Your direction. Amen.

BASED ON PSALM 139:14–16 (MSG)

4

A WORD TO FATHERS

Never Underestimate Your Impact

Not much was happening out in left field this particular Saturday afternoon. The action was taking place inside the diamond—as usual. This was my third year playing Little League baseball. And I was bored—as usual.

The Jaycees, our biggest rival, were at bat when our coach stepped onto the field to request a time-out. This seldom happened, so I knew something big was up. Usually when Coach stepped onto the field, it was to have a private powwow with our pitcher. All of the coolest infield guys joined Coach at the mound. I had never been asked to join and often wondered what a private conversation with Coach was like.

My dream was about to come true. As Coach continued to wave players in, I realized he was motioning my way. I couldn't believe it—Coach was asking me to join him at Baseball Mecca! My heart pounded as I raced toward the mound.

Coach shooed away the rest of the players. It was just him and me. In my mind flashed images of a special play. Coach was about to ask me (undoubtedly his best left fielder) for something really big. I was going to save the team. What Little League–playing, cleat-wearing Reggie Jackson wannabe hasn't dreamed of a moment such as this?

Coach put his arm around my shoulder. Then he said it—the one sentence that brought me back to reality: "Jeffrey, the press box called down and said you need to quit digging holes in the outfield with your cleats."

So much for a top-secret play. I stumbled back to left field and covered my holes, crushed.

Through the years, this story has provided many a laugh around our family dinner table. But the most memorable part of the story for me has never been what happened at the mound. Feeling disappointed and embarrassed from the experience, I turned back toward the stands to see my father, as I did several times throughout each game. Sure enough, there he sat, giving me the nod that said, "Keep going, son." In that moment of personal shame, having my father's approval and support made nothing else matter.

It's hard to find words to describe the feeling that came over me at seeing my father sitting in the stands week after week and watching me play ball. From left field I could seldom hear his voice, but his presence at each game and his interest in something important to me spoke volumes. *I believe in you*—that was the "sound" I heard loud and clear.

In this chapter, I want to talk specifically to dads. I'll speak specifically to moms in the next chapter. (Moms and dads, feel free to read both chapters.) Dad, as you read this chapter, I want you to think about those four important words you can tell your teen: "I believe in you." I wholeheartedly believe those four words are what this generation's teens desperately desire to hear from their fathers. Saying those four words is the basis for having a positive impact on your teen's life.

What Dads Can Do

Your teen needs to know you believe in him or her no matter what. How do you express that? Let me suggest eight ways:

1. Lead the Spiritual Climb

Maybe you've heard this before: a man is supposed to be the spiritual leader in the family. A father's job is to take the initiative in bringing his family closer to God. But how does that happen? It starts with you. It's as simple as that.

Maybe your life seems too busy for that. And it's true—as a man, you are responsible for much. If you are anything like me, your days feel too short, and your responsibilities feel too great.

But the key to your relationship with God is *making time* to be alone with Him. In Matthew 14:23 we read, "[Jesus] went up on a mountainside by himself to pray." If the Savior of the world needed time alone with God, then how much more does each of us need time with God? I encourage you to take time consistently to get away and climb the mountain—find your place, find your time, find your way, and get alone with God. As you spend time alone with God and in His Word, He will better prepare you to be a great leader in your home.

Here's something practical—I call it the 1:1:1 Plan. Spend a minimum of one hour a week, one day (or Saturday afternoon) a month, and one weekend a year alone with God.

Imagine the impact you could have upon your family by implementing the 1:1:1 Plan in your life. Plan into your schedule consistent time to listen to God, refocus your priorities, reenergize your commitment as a father, reaffirm your life purpose, and retune your heart's ear to God's voice.

Here's something else practical. As the spiritual leader of your family, you need to make prayer a priority in your home, not just something you do in a moment of tragedy, at church, or before carving the turkey at Christmas. Let your teen see that you are a man of prayer. Pray during times of personal joy and family successes as well as when something good happens in the life of a family member. That means you say something like, "Okay, everybody, let's pray…" (or whatever fits your personality). You might get some funny looks at first, but try it.

Don't feel guilty over what you haven't done in the past (think Sweeping Aside Motion). Don't feel intimidated over the fear of not doing it right. Just step up to the plate and swing big.

2. Establish the Right Atmosphere

As a dad, you have the job of establishing the atmosphere in your home. And in part, this means determining what comes into your home. Christian books, videos, and games can help to set the right climate of spiritual living for your teen. Find a book at a Christian bookstore that offers you weekly devotional suggestions and outlines. Watch a movie together as a family and discuss the worldview being depicted. Play a board game or shoot pool and pray before you break for the night. The key is to create an environment that is relevant and relational, one which will encourage your family to pursue a deeper walk with God.

Another part of establishing the right family atmosphere is making sure your teen sees that church is an important part of your family's life. It is good for your teen to go to church. But it is even better for your teen to go to church *with you*. Of course, this is often easier said than done.

One parent wrote me to say, "My daughter thinks that church is boring. She's given it a try, but she doesn't like the youth group and says that the other teens ignore her. Should I let her stay home, or should I make her go anyway?"

My answer: maybe one, maybe the other.

I hear this complaint often from teens. Some use such a statement as an excuse to sleep in on Sundays. For others, it is a legitimate issue. You may need to take a serious look at the authenticity and effectiveness of your church's youth program.

I encourage you not to force church upon your teen but instead take action in positive ways. Talk with adult volunteers in the youth department. Take your youth pastor out for coffee. If they are unresponsive to your concerns or you are unsatisfied with what you discover, and if your teen continues to say he or she does not feel fed in the present worship environment, you may need to take extreme measures.

I am not suggesting that every parent whose teen complains about a place of worship should simply find a new one. Only after much consideration, prayer, and confirmation from God should such a step ever be taken. But I am also not opposed to this if it is in the best interest of your teen and if it will encourage your teen to explore a deeper relationship with God in a different church environment. The key is to find a Bible-believing church where you feel led to serve as a family and to consistently attend, then to go home and do something together, such as grabbing some chicken wings on the way, hitting Play on the TiVo, and watching a favorite show or movie.

3. Take Charge in Communication

One of the greatest ways you can show your teen "I believe in you" is by communicating regularly. Your teen may not initiate such communication, particularly when it comes to talking about deep subjects, so it's up to you to bring up the serious stuff. If you do not talk with your teen about the hard issues of life, who will?

Talking about things such as sex, substance abuse, school life, and peer pressure may not be the easiest and most comfortable conversations you have with your teen. But what's important here is not how comfortable you are; it's that your teen feels your solid impact in his or her life.

Sixteen-year-old Stephen said this to me: "I have been struggling with lust since I was in eighth grade. It's embarrassing, and I don't know what to do. My dad is so involved at church—he probably would die if I ever talked to him about all of this. But I wish I could."

Make it a priority to spend at least ten minutes a day in relevant communication with your teen. Relevant communication can happen wherever and whenever—while playing ball, working in the yard, driving in the car, or just watching TV. Maybe your teen won't talk at first, but most likely, when you least expect it, your teen will open up.

4. Invest Time

Consistently take time to get away from work, school, and home and hang out with your teen. Pick a night once a week, or biweekly, or just whenever you feel like it, and go and have fun. See a movie. Play basketball. Ride go-carts. Go hiking, swim, shop, ski, hunt, play golf, or throw darts. Whatever your teen would love.

When I ask teens for one way they would improve their relationships with their dads if they could, they overwhelmingly say, "Spend more time together."

Have you ever said anything like this?

- "It's just this one time to be away. I know I already promised my son I'd be there, but this meeting out of town could make or break my career."

- "I don't need to spend time with my kids in the Word. I'm tired tonight. Plus, isn't that why our church hired a youth pastor?"
- "I'd better not ask my daughter too many questions about who she's going out with tonight and where they're going. She may think I'm being nosy. If she wants to talk, she'll come to me."
- "I'd better not bring up that subject with my son. He'll figure it out on his own. I did, right?"

Why prioritize spending time with your teen? Because time leads to communication. And communication leads to having a positive impact in your teen's life.

5. Teach Respect to Your Son

Many media images today show people disrespecting one another. People work out their differences by insults and putdowns. This is particularly true of guys—guys are taught to be jerks to one another and to women. And in such an environment, I can think of no greater example to model for your teen than the one carried out by Jesus on the cross.

John 19:25–27 reads, "Near the cross of Jesus stood his mother.... When Jesus saw his mother there, and the disciple whom he loved standing nearby, he said to his mother, 'Dear woman, here is your son,' and to the disciple, 'Here is your mother.' From that time on, this disciple took her into his home."

In other words, after having been beaten, spit on, stripped of His clothes, cursed at, slapped, kicked, mocked, ridiculed, and then nailed to a cross, and within moments of breathing His last breath, Jesus was more concerned about His mother than about His own personal pain. What an incredible act and example for all men!

Jesus made respect cool that day. As a father, you can help your teen see that respect is still cool today, particularly when it comes to respecting women.

I remember well the first few months of dating my future wife. Amy's father spoke to me one evening as she and I were leaving for a date: "Jeffrey, protect her tonight. She is my only daughter." I have never forgotten the overwhelming sense of responsibility that I took upon myself that night after hearing these words from him.

The same is true of your son and the young women in his life. Not only is it his responsibility to model Jesus's actions by respecting the women with whom he comes in contact, but it is also his responsibility to protect them. For instance, on a date, it is your son's responsibility to respect and protect his date by never placing her in any environment where there is the potential for something dangerous to happen. This means never parking somewhere alone, being careful about the movie they watch, never going to a party where there are drugs and alcohol, and more.

Does your son know this?

6. Teach True Security to Your Daughter

When my daughter Bailey was five, she gave me a birthday card she had made herself. The card read:

> Dear Daddy,
>   Bailey loves you very much. I will always be your best friend forever. Even when I am older, I will always love you and be your best friend.
>   Love, Bailey

I'm going to remind her of this card when she turns sixteen. I'll probably have the card laminated before she hits junior high school so I can wear it around my neck every time her friends come over.

At her young age today, Bailey still relies on me to help her feel secure. She wants affirmation when she draws a picture. She wants me to celebrate her successes in school. She longs for me to tell her how beautiful she is. She loves it when I pray with her. If she ever falls off her bike, she wants me right there beside her to comfort her. She has given me the distinct pleasure of occupying a special space in her heart.

Do you remember such moments with your daughter? Believe it or not, even when she's a teen, you are still her hero. She may not tell you or run and jump into your arms like she once did. But she still needs you to make her feel special, secure, and significant. She still needs you to say with your life, your time, and your involvement, "I believe in you."

In a world of confusing and often misleading messages, teen girls are persuaded to fit the mold, have the look, build the body, and get the guy. Here are a few of the lies Satan uses to get into your daughter's heart:

- To be popular with the boys, you need to dress sexy.
- Only skinny girls are loved. Go ahead and purge.
- You absolutely must have a boyfriend to feel secure.
- Never talk to your parents about anything. They won't understand.

What's a dad to do?

First, realize your teen daughter still needs you. Even if she never tells you so anymore, she needs you involved in her life.

Second, develop a game plan for involvement. You know your daughter. You know her likes and dislikes. You know her favorite foods, her favorite rock stars, her favorite genre of music, her favorite movies, her favorite store to shop at, and a whole lot more. (Hint: If you don't, ask her mom.) Now, take the knowledge you have and make it work for you.

One father told me he did this. "One night a month is just for me and Kiley. We go out, we eat, and we see a movie or go watch a game. We grab coffee and we make a date of it. I'll admit it was a little awkward for us both at first. But we've been doing this for two years now, and we've never been closer. She talks to me and shares things with me that I never dreamed she would. She has this place in her life that she lets me into. She leaves for college this year, and I will cherish forever these past two years spending time together."

What if it doesn't go as smoothly as this for you? Start slowly. Build trust one step at a time. Ask your daughter what she would like to do. And let your teen know that you just want to take some time to be together. Maybe it's something like this:

- creating a date night once a month or week where you go out for ice cream
- asking her how her day went
- writing her a letter telling her what she means to you
- telling her she's beautiful
- hugging her

As a father, you play a critical role in the process of helping your daughter feel loved, needed, and secure. Live a life before her that says, "I believe in you." You will help her not get lost in all the lies.

7. Use Words Wisely

Earlier I talked about playing baseball. Truthfully, I was a terrible athlete. I played two years of football, five years of baseball, and eleven years of basketball. And while I don't know the stats, trust me that there were plenty of fumbles, missed catches, dropped pop-ups, strikeouts, and air balls.

Here's the cool thing—from the first time my dad saw me hold a baseball bat, he had to know that I probably would never make it into the National Baseball Hall of Fame unless I purchased a ticket. Even so, I knew my dad was proud of me. How did I know? He told me so.

Your teen greatly desires to know and feel that you are proud of him or her. It's not about your teen's ability. Your teen needs and wants a real connection with you that goes far beyond any gift, talent, or ability he or she may possess in the classroom or on the court, field, or stage.

If your teen is an athlete, it is important that you solidify the truth that your love is not conditioned on his or her performance on the field. Teens with athletic abilities are often praised for their achievements. But what happens when their achievements do not measure up to the expected or desired standards? There is obviously nothing wrong with encouraging and challenging your teen to be the best at any task faced. But it must also be clear that no matter what happens in the game, you are well pleased with your teen.

This leads to another issue: what about teens who have no interest in playing sports? Society sends a powerful message to today's teens about their value being directly related to their athletic ability. But many teens have amazing abilities in areas of life other than sports. Your teen needs to know that it is okay if he or she chooses not to be a jock. Have you told your teen this?

8. Be the Reassurance Your Teen Needs

Remember when your child was young and had a nightmare? He or she shuffled into your bedroom in footie p.j.'s, asking you to slay the bogeyman under the bed. You were the Fear Killer back then, and nothing could hurt your child when you were around.

Your teen needs you to provide the same sort of rock-solid reassurance today. It's probably not about bogeyman nightmares anymore. But your teen still must fight fears.

Rebecca, fifteen, recently told me: "I live with fear every day. I want to talk with my dad about it, but I'm not sure he will get it. I wish for one day he could feel my fears, then he would understand what I live with."

There are so many teens just like Rebecca who live with constant fear. Maybe it's the fear of not having the newest, coolest stuff like "everyone else." Maybe it's the fear of rejection, betrayal, or loneliness. Some teens fear they will lose their present family structure through the death of a loved one or their parents' divorce. Others fear failing, being different, being laughed at by friends, or not mattering to others. These kinds of fears and more are real for many teens.

Teens also have fears that you might not expect. I heard one teen say, "I love it when Mom lets us have a party at our house. This way, I know certain things aren't going to happen in our home that I might be tempted to do while in my friends' homes."

Another teen said, "My spiritual life could really sink when I graduate and move away to college. Without my parents to get me out of bed on Sunday mornings, I'll probably have a hard time getting up for church."

Both of these teens were saying, "I am fearful of what choices I might make when tempted while away from my parents."

Do you know what your teen fears most? Have you ever talked to your teen about his or her fears? Start talking. Help your teen sort through his or her feelings. Provide the support and reassurance your teen needs.

The Call of a Father

Dad, Satan is working overtime to convince you that your role isn't needed now that your son or daughter has reached the teen years. Satan and his demons want you to believe that everything else is more important than your teen—your status within your community, your friendships, your job. But the fact is, nothing is more important than the impact you have upon your teen's life.

You have a God-ordained call upon your life to be a father to your children. Maybe life feels out of control for you. Maybe you're more distant from your child than ever before. Maybe you feel you can never become the father your teen needs. Maybe you think it is too late to win back your teen. But if you believe these lies, then the Enemy has you exactly where he wants you—ready to turn and run, ready to surrender. Your teen needs you to head back into the battle and fight in your role as a father. You can do it. You can seize this moment, become the father of impact you were born to be, and win!

Praying Scripture for Your Teen

Lord, help me to be the father I need to be. Help me to meet with You often. Be my Guide. Help me to lead my teen in the way this child should go. I claim this verse as Your promise to me in this area: "I can do everything through him who gives me strength." Amen.

BASED ON PHILIPPIANS 4:13

5

A WORD TO MOTHERS

Your Vital Role

I remember so many special moments from my childhood and adolescence. I remember the spring when we had a tremendous amount of rain and the streets in front of our house flooded. I can still see my brother and me running through the streets barefoot, playing chase in floodwaters up to our knees. For some reason, all we wore was our underwear. (I'm not sure why; it's a little embarrassing as I think about it today.)

I remember a broken finger in first grade, a broken arm in second grade, and the terrible skateboard wreck I had in sixth grade. I remember, too, my first car wreck. I was fourteen. I didn't have a license. It wasn't my car. And that's all I will tell you about it.

I remember my first baseball practice at the Boys & Girls Club in Pine Bluff, Arkansas. I remember countless basketball, football, and baseball games in the years to follow.

I remember having horrific nightmares as a kid. I don't remember what they were about; I just remember waking up and feeling terrified.

I remember my younger brother being born the night of my seventh birthday. I was happy and excited and scared all at the same time. I knew that life had just changed, and I wasn't sure how I would like my new brother at first.

I remember the Christmas I got a go-cart and an Atari. I was sure no kid could possibly want anything but those wonderful presents.

I remember watching *The Cosby Show* every Thursday night. I remember Heathcliff's funky, colorful sweaters and thinking how cool it would be to live in a brownstone in New York. And I remember wondering if families ever actually held funerals around the toilet like the Huxtables did when Rudy's pet fish Lamont died.

I remember singing in the talent show at our high school. I was a freshman and sang a Barry Manilow song. I've been trying to forget that experience ever since.

I remember my first date, my first kiss, my first love, and my first breakup. I remember so much more about growing up. I could go on and on.

What was the common thread in each of those special moments? When it comes to every ball game, every skinned knee and elbow, every celebration and every tragedy, every report card, and every breakup, I remember Mom being there. She was there to comfort and talk. To encourage and confide in. To listen and speak and laugh and cry with.

It's not that Mom coddled me or that I was a mama's boy. It's that her presence built godly strength into my life. Now that I'm an adult, my mother and I don't live in the same city, and I don't see her every day anymore, but not a day goes by that I don't lean into the influence she provided. I know I am the person of character I am today, in part, because of my mom.

Would you like to be the kind of mother who positively shapes character in your teen's life? Mom, this whole book is written with you in mind, and in this chapter we're going to look at some of the specific ways you can support your teen in today's culture war. You are on the front lines with your teen. And God has a special calling for you in this fight.

Just for Moms

It doesn't matter if you're a stay-at-home mother or if you work outside the home; chances are good that you carry the load of the hands-on interaction with your kids. You're in the kitchen more when they want to talk. You keep a more watchful eye on their daily interactions. You drive them to and from soccer and dance practice. You buy their toothpaste and deodorant and know what size gym shoes they wear. It isn't that fathers never know what's going on; it's just that mothers seem to have a special bond with their children, an intuition that keeps them in touch with the kids in ways their spouses aren't.

A mother's role is often far from glamorous. Because of the day-to-day interaction, it seems that mothers often get the dirty work when it comes to raising teens. You're around your kids more, so they become more familiar with you. Maybe you find that you get brushed off more or teased more or talked back to more. It seems that many of the teens I've talked with take their moms for granted. When I asked them directly about this, here's what some of them had to say:

> Sure, Mom does a lot for me. I probably don't appreciate her as much as I should. (Grayson, seventeen)

It seems like I can get away with more stuff with my mom. Dad's always serious. It's like if he puts his foot down, we know he really means it. But with Mom, we can kind of push her to the limit. (Jasmine, fourteen)

My dad's at work all day, so I only see him at nights. He travels, too, so it's not like he's around much. Mom is there for me when I get home from school, so I'm just with her more. (Megan, fifteen)

Mom had this chart she made for us to keep track of our chores and stuff. But it didn't last very long because me and my brother started making fun of it. So after a while she said "whatever" and that was the end of the chart. (Wyatt, thirteen)

My mom's the greatest. She's a dental assistant and has flexible hours, so she's home a lot. If I ever need something, I talk to Mom. (Sienna, fifteen)

What's the encouragement here? When your kids are teens, you may not always get the appreciation you deserve, but there's a good chance that all the hard work will pay off in years to come. Sometimes your children will articulate how much they appreciate you only when they become adults. Other times they may never say anything, but you (and your spouse) will have the satisfaction of knowing you rose to the incredibly hard and yet rewarding challenge of being a mother.

Consider the godly mothering that was demonstrated by Hannah, the mother of Samuel, the man who eventually became one of Israel's greatest prophets. Even before Samuel was born, Hannah was fighting for her son in prayer in ways different from her husband. (Or at least his prayers are never mentioned in the Bible.)

It's an incredible story (see 1 Samuel 1:1–2:11, 18–21). Hannah was unable to have children. This was considered a disgrace in that culture. For years she dreamed, hoped, and prayed for a baby. Finally God answered her prayer, and Hannah conceived. It was a son. Her hope was at last fulfilled. But here's where the story takes a twist. After the child was weaned, Hannah made good on a promise that she had made to God before Samuel was born. Hannah took her young son to the temple, where she dedicated him to God. Then she did what must have taken incredible courage—she left her young son there. From that moment on, Samuel was raised at the temple by the priest Eli.

No one is saying that you need to take your child to church, dedicate him to God, and leave him there for the rest of his life to be raised by the pastor's family. But this story shows some strong examples of things moms can do to fight for their kids. It's not that fathers can't do these things. Yet what's interesting is that the story shows a mother doing them.

Perhaps it's hard to think of yourself as a fighter. Moms are supposed to be the scraped-knee bandagers. The cookie bakers. The den vacuumers and blind dusters. But this story shows Hannah doing battle!

How a Mother Fights

Let's take a look at a few of the distinctives of Hannah's fighting style. She lived thousands of years ago, but God's truth is always relevant. By looking at Hannah's life, we can learn important truths about what it means to help teens through the battles in today's culture.

A Mother Fights by Prayer

Hannah had a battle on her hands. For years, things weren't going her way in her personal life. Her husband's other wife, Peninnah, ridiculed Hannah because she had been unable to conceive children. Satan was undoubtedly working hard to discourage Hannah and convince her that God would not grant her the desires of her heart.

But Hannah fought back. Her main weapon, her Ultimate Power Stance, was prayer. She never gave up on God. She believed that God could answer prayer, and she resolved to give her situation over to Him.

A MOTHER'S PRAYERS FOR HER TEEN

Here are ten specific ways you can pray for your teen every day. Write down this list, and keep it someplace where you can see it. Use the list as a reminder to fight for your teen in prayer daily.

Lord, this day, as every day, I pray for _____. [Write your child's name here and in all the blanks to come.] I pray…

1. For _____'s salvation [if your teen is not a believer] and continued walk with the Lord [if your child is].

2. For God's protection and safety for _____ and his/her friends.

3. For strength for _____ to take a stand for what is right when in a moment of temptation.

4. That God will provide _____ with

Maybe you are at a place in your life right now where it seems that your timing and God's aren't in sync. Maybe you find yourself in distress over what appear to be unanswered prayers to God concerning your life or the life of your teen. Hannah's story is a reminder that God's timing is never wrong.

Even though Hannah couldn't see it, God's plan was being played out exactly as He desired in Hannah's life. What I love about this story is that even though Hannah couldn't see the big picture, she still believed that God was in full control. Did she like the situation? Absolutely not!

a godly spouse someday and that he/she would make wise choices in his/her dating life in the meantime. I pray right now for my child's future spouse—for his/her safety, protection, purity, guidance, and wise choices. Lord, You know who this person is even though I might not.

5. For godly friendships for _____.

6. That _____ would have opportunities to share Jesus with those who don't know Him.

7. For wisdom and discernment for _____ and for his/her friends.

8. That God would use _____ mightily for His glory.

9. That _____ would honor God in his or her private life.

10. For clear direction for _____ in life after high school.

Scripture tells us that she was "desperately unhappy and in such pain" (1 Samuel 1:16, MSG). But even in her anguish she continually went to God in prayer.

Time spent with God in prayer is critical to winning the many battles we face personally and for our children. Scripture confirms this. Psalm 34:17 says, "The righteous cry out, and the LORD hears them; he delivers them from all their troubles." Along the same lines, 1 John 5:14–15 says, "Now this is the confidence we have before Him: whenever we ask anything according to His will, He hears us. And if we know that He hears whatever we ask, we know that we have what we have asked Him for" (HCSB).

No matter what circumstance you are facing in your own life or with your teen, the example of Hannah shows that you can find confidence in knowing that God has everything under control. Use your own Ultimate Power Stance. Fight for your teen every day in prayer!

A Mother Fights for Integrity

Year after year, Hannah endured the jeers of her husband's other wife. Hannah could have been a bitter woman. But she wasn't. She rejoiced in her son's birth and then, as a true woman of integrity, stood by her word. Hannah did what she promised she would do and took her son to the temple to live, even though it was the hard thing to do. She gave up the one thing she wanted most in life.

Having integrity means being devoted to doing what's right. Yet have you ever wondered where integrity has gone in today's culture? Look at a few e-mails I've recently received.

A fourteen-year-old boy e-mailed: "Jeffrey, I look at porn almost every night on my computer in my room. The funny thing is, I'm basically okay with it. I'm not concerned that what I'm doing is wrong, because what I'm doing works for me. What else am I supposed to do at this age? I believe that God is okay with my lifestyle because it doesn't harm anybody. Isn't that what morals are about—not hurting anybody else?"

An eighth-grade girl wrote in response to a question I asked her in a previous e-mail: "Yeah, I've cheated a few times. But what's the big deal? It's just a lousy test, and doesn't everybody do it from time to time?"

A sixteen-year-old boy wrote: "I've taken my Honda up to 125 mph on the street—and I think it will go faster. All my friends are into street racing and seeing how fast we can get our cars to go. There's a side of me that knows this is wrong, but laws are meant to be broken. Isn't that what Jesus did?"

The problem with these three e-mails is that they are all redefining integrity. These teens are essentially saying, "Look, as long as I can justify what I'm doing, then what I'm doing is okay." It's part of that trend of relativism we talked about a few chapters back.

Adhering to the idea of high moral principles regardless of the circumstance is a lifestyle choice that many teens are completely ignorant of or defiant about. But it is one that you as a mom can push your teen toward.

When the time and context are right in a conversation, take your teen to Scripture. Your teen needs to hear and see, and see consistently from you, that integrity is essential to living a life that honors God. As Proverbs 10:9 says, "The man of integrity walks securely, but he who takes crooked paths will be found out."

A Mother Fights for Time

After leaving Samuel in the care of the priest Eli, Hannah no longer saw her son each day. But we know that she was still active in his life as much as she was able. The Bible tells us in 1 Samuel 2:19 that "his mother made him a little robe and took it to him when she went up with her husband to offer the annual sacrifice." Hannah was still committed to her son. This took discipline, especially since God blessed Hannah with five more children and she was no doubt busy taking care of them.

How much time do you spend with your teen? If your schedule is like mine, then probably not as much as you would like. One of the biggest ways the Enemy fights to steal your teen away is by convincing your family that it is okay to fill the calendar, as long as what you are filling the calendar with is good. A packed calendar is the number one excuse parents share with me to explain why they do not spend more time with their teens.

As a mom of discipline, you must maintain calendar control for your family. There is a huge difference between being involved with your teen and being busy in the life of your teen. As a mom, you have to draw the line when enough has become enough.

I'm all for allowing kids to enjoy activities in life that are important to them. But there will come a point (sooner than you can imagine) when your teen will no longer live in your home. You thus have a small window of opportunity to impact your teen's life in the areas that matter most. This is why calendar control must be an area of no compromise.

If you need to regain schedule sanity for your family, establish a plan with your husband, and then have a family meeting to discuss your new strategy. Don't be surprised if your teen responds unfavorably at first. As a matter of fact, if you've given your teen free rein in the past with his or her calendar, expect it. But stay the course. *No* is not always the easiest word to use, but it is often the best word for you to use when you take control of the calendar.

And as you go to work in this area of your family life, get ready for temptation. As you commit to control the calendar, Satan will try to take you for a ride down Guilt Trip Highway. He will try to convince you that saying yes "just this one time" will be okay. If you choose not to, he will do everything within his power to make you feel guilty for saying no. Don't let him win! Saying no to another activity on your calendar is actually saying yes to time with your teen.

A Mother Fights for a Legacy

Even before my daughters were born, it was my prayer that God would use my children to do remarkable things for Him. This is what Hannah prayed for her son in 1 Samuel 1:27–28 : "I prayed for this child, and the LORD has granted me what I asked of him. So now I give him to the LORD. For his whole life he will be given over to the LORD."

When Hannah prayed, "I give him to the LORD," she was praying that Samuel would leave a legacy worth remembering for generations to come. And look at what the Bible says about the legacy this man left: "Samuel grew up. GOD was with him, and Samuel's prophetic record was flawless. Everyone in Israel, from Dan in the north to Beersheba in the south, recognized that Samuel was the real thing—a true prophet of GOD" (1 Samuel 3:19–20, MSG).

Samuel found favor with God and left a legacy truly worth remembering. Isn't this what we as parents desire most for our children? I know this is one of *my* greatest aspirations with my daughters: to see Bailey and Brynnan write such a legacy with their lives. So I ask myself, *How can my girls find such genuine favor with God and ultimately leave a legacy of significance?*

There is no greater legacy a parent could desire to leave than that of a child who learns to truly worship God. Because of Hannah's obedience and faithfulness to God, she wrote a legacy with her own life that influenced Samuel into becoming a man who worshiped God with his life. One legacy produces another.

On the other hand, a teen whose parents are not committed to God isn't automatically excluded from living a life surrendered to Him. For instance, consider a fourteen-year-old named Christopher who used to be my neighbor. He is the only son of a single mother. Christopher's father had not been actively involved in his life since Christopher was four.

Often, during a game of 21 in my driveway, Christopher and I would talk about what was going on in his world. I remember one particular day when we were shooting ball in the driveway and I was actually winning, which was rare. I knew something was weighing heavily on Christopher's mind, so I asked him what was up.

Almost immediately he said, "You know my mom has a new boyfriend?" (I had recently met the new man in her life.) "Most Friday nights he spends the night at our house. This isn't right, is it?"

I knew Christopher's mom well. With no financial help from Christopher's father, she worked a full-time job, drove Christopher to and from school, aimed to stay involved in activities important to her son, and attended every baseball, football, and basketball game he played in. I knew this left her with minimal personal time. She had the tough responsibility of raising a teenage son all by herself. She was a Christian, consistently took Christopher to church, and told me on several occasions that she did not want to see Christopher make the same wrong choices his father had made. She wanted the best for Christopher. But in spite of all the good things she was doing for him, she was sending him the message loud and clear that her personal life was off-limits to God.

Christopher was watching. And he was learning much from what he saw.

What is your teen learning from what he or she sees in your life? When you fight for integrity in your teen's life, a huge part of the fight is maintaining integrity in your life as well. This goes for both parents, not only mothers.

A Mother Fights for Surrender

By bringing her son to the temple, Hannah demonstrated complete faith that Samuel was in God's hands and that God would do as He desired with him.

Hannah's desire to honor God superseded her desire to hold on to her son. Her example shows us that the greatest joy in having children lies in being willing to give our children back to God. Even before Samuel took his first breath, Hannah was at peace with the one thing that all mothers must be willing to do at some point: let go.

Now, this doesn't mean that Hannah simply dropped Samuel off with a twenty-four pack of Huggies and some wet wipes and said, "See ya!" She was still active and involved in Samuel's life, doing her part to provide for him as a mother.

But Hannah carried out one vital act essential for us as parents to grasp and emulate. It's surrender. By returning her son to God, Hannah was proclaiming her trust in God's goodness. She was proclaiming that she believed God could do more in her son's life than she could ever do on her own. And Hannah trusted that whatever God chose to do with Samuel's life, God had it all figured out.

Is there something you, too, need to surrender to God? The loss of a loved one? Bitterness over a divorce? Hurt from something that someone said or did to you? Guilt from your past? Your teen's decision to embrace a prodigal life? It could be that, just as with Hannah, God is inviting you to a place of surrender, a place where you are willing to step out and trust Him even though it doesn't make sense to you. God is good. It makes sense to Him.

Mom's Battle Checklist

In the days ahead, consider sharing with your teen that you understand what he or she is going through. Share stories about how you struggled as a teen. Share your desire to help your teen see past the lies of Satan and never compromise, no matter how great the desire to do so. Show your teen the foundations of God's promises to those who obey Him, as found in Deuteronomy 28:11–13:

> The LORD will grant you abundant prosperity—in the fruit of your womb, the young of your livestock and the crops of your ground—in the land he swore to your forefathers to give you.
>
> The LORD will open the heavens, the storehouse of his bounty, to send rain on your land in season and to bless all the work of your hands. You will lend to many nations but will borrow from none. The LORD will make you the head, not the tail. If you pay attention to the commands of the LORD your God that I give you this day and carefully follow them, you will always be at the top, never at the bottom.

Mom, God is inviting you to powerfully shape your teen's character. Your role can be a difficult one, but it is also a privileged one. Your calling is to be on the front lines with your teen, guiding him or her in today's culture war. God has a special calling for you in this fight.

Praying Scripture for Your Teen

Father, You say in Your Word that even children are known by their actions, by whether their conduct is pure and right. I pray that my teen would be a person of integrity. I pray that my son will be like a well-nurtured plant or my daughter will be like a pillar carved to adorn a palace. I pray that my teen would know the holy Scriptures, which are able to make this child wise for salvation through faith in Christ Jesus. Help me be the mother I need to be. Amen.

BASED ON PROVERBS 20:11, PSALM 144:12,
AND 2 TIMOTHY 3:15

PART 2

THE ISSUES THAT AFFECT YOUR TEEN MOST

6

THE STRUGGLE TO COMMUNICATE

How to Talk to Your Teen About Anything

Communication isn't always easy or fun, especially with a teen. I doubt that you need me to convince you of this. One mom told me, "I'm tired of even trying to talk with my teen. Every time I try to talk to him, he acts as though he wants nothing to do with me."

If you can relate to this mom, you are not alone. Your teen may not fully understand that he or she is wired by God to rely on you. But this is truth. And you must hold on to this truth, especially if the lines of communication are stretched to the point of breaking.

Have you ever considered this issue from your teen's perspective? Remember what it was like to be a teen? Were you always able to talk with your parents? Here's what a few of today's teens told me about their struggles with communication:

> It means so much to me when my dad talks to me. I know he's a busy guy, but I actually like hearing what he has to say. Sometimes he's really funny too. (Cameron, eighteen)

Just once I wish my mom would ask my opinion about something. She always gives me advice, but she never asks what I think about anything. I've got good things to say too. (Brooke, sixteen)

Nobody talks to anybody in my house. The TV is always on. My mom says not to interrupt her during her shows. My dad has to watch the news every night. Then he watches it again on another channel. Then he reads the newspaper. Then he goes to bed. (Blake, fifteen)

Once I tried telling my mother about this joke I pulled on my friend Jake. But I don't think she got it. She just stood there with her mouth open and then told me I needed to apologize to Jake. Boy, that's the last time I tell her anything. (Micah, sixteen)

My mom is not afraid to say hard things to me. I like that about her, even though I don't show it sometimes. (Lucy, fourteen)

When I ask teens to identify one aspect they would like most to improve about their relationships with their moms and dads, overwhelmingly teens mention communication. Effective communication with your teen is a precious skill and necessary tool in helping your teen navigate these years and fight the daily war being waged for his or her soul.

The Two Ps

When it comes to communication, there are countless issues and scenarios that can leave you and your teen frustrated, angry, and resentful of each other. Have you ever said to yourself things like this?

- *My teen just won't listen to me. I don't know what's going on in his life.*
- *I don't want to be a nag. I'd better just lay off and keep quiet for a while.*
- *If I talk to her about how she dresses, she'll think I'm old-fashioned and uncool.*
- *I've tried to talk to him before about the music he listens to, but he won't listen. I'm through with trying.*

Talking—and listening—to a teen can be hard work. But you can do it. God has called you to this role. A little later in the chapter, we'll look at some specific communication techniques. But first let's look at two vital, overarching practices that help to establish strong communication with your teen.

1. Prepare

Preparation is an integral step toward improved communication. Taking time before you talk may be just what you need to organize your thoughts and help you develop a plan of action.

Remember the Sweeping Aside Motion. This is not a time to beat up on yourself if you have not communicated in the past with your teen as you have desired. This *is* a time for you to better prepare yourself. Taking the time to prepare your thoughts will help you to take full advantage of a door of opportunity for communication when it begins to open.

The rule of thumb here is to know what you want to say—and why you want to say it—before you say it. Ask yourself questions such as these:

- *If conversations in the past have ended poorly, what might I modify about my approach?*

- *Is there a specific topic I need to approach with my teen but have been avoiding?*
- *Has God placed a burden on my heart that He wants me to discuss with my teen, but as of yet, I have not? If so, how will I accomplish this? When? Where?*
- *If I want to say something to my teen, what is my interest in doing so? What's the goal here?*

2. Pray

God has called you to be a parent ready and willing to communicate His truths to your teen. At the same time, Satan is fighting to convince you that you are neither worthy nor capable of this calling.

I met one dad who said, "My son and I barely talk these days. I don't know how it got out of control. But we hardly know each other anymore. I used to be his biggest hero. I know I've failed, and I'm not sure how to win him back."

If you are having a similarly difficult time communicating with your teen, stop right now and take your communication concerns to God. This is exactly what Moses did when God called him to speak to Pharaoh. Moses didn't shy away from bringing his fears before God (see Exodus 3:1–4:17).

Your situation is no surprise to God. He wants you to know that no matter how difficult or discouraging it all is, He has a plan to use you as a voice of truth to speak into the life of your teen.

Perhaps the lines of communication between you and your teen *are* working right now. Great! But hold on, because you, too, are marked. Evil spirits work overtime to disrupt your relationship with your teen. In just one conflict, they could turn the whole relationship upside down.

Wherever your relationship with your teen is right now, you must continue to make prayer a part of your battle plan to strengthen and protect that relationship. Assume your Ultimate Power Stance, and pray specifically that God will:

- teach you what to say, just as God promised Moses in Exodus 4
- give you discernment to say the right things at the right time
- protect your relationship with your teen, so that your teen turns to you when facing struggles, questions, and dilemmas

Just as God gave Moses the words to speak before Pharaoh, so He can give you the words to speak to your teen. Ask God for help, get ready, and watch what He does!

Communication Strategies

Successful communication involves countless issues, depending on your situation. Tailoring a specific plan of action can help, especially when dealing with difficult or sensitive issues. The following ten strategies can help you develop a successful plan for healthy communication.

1. Schedule Your Teen into Your Day

I know plenty of busy parents who literally plan "meetings" with their teens. These parents write their teens' names into their Day-Timers or schedule them into their PDAs. These parents take advantage of communication opportunities (even if they are brief) such as at breakfast, during the ride home after school, when their teens come through the door after practice or work, or right before bedtime.

It may take a little experimentation and persistence, but work to find those moments in each day when your teen is most apt to talk. Get these times on your daily calendar and live by them. They could be the most valuable minutes of your day—and your teen's!

2. Start with Talking About Little Things

Ten minutes of daily small talk can go far when building a broader level of trust with your teen. What interests your teen? Sports? Music? Friends? Hobbies? Start there. As your teen sees that you are interested in the little things in his or her life, your teen will begin to trust you more when it comes to the bigger issues.

3. Choose a Relaxed Environment for Your Teen

When you've got something important to discuss with your teen, a successful talk can often depend upon a relaxed environment. One mom told me that her son loves music. A great way to get him talking about his day, his dating life, and more is to turn on the music he likes.

Where is your teen most relaxed? Watching a ball game? Playing video games? Spending a day on the boat with you? Helping to create an environment that is comfortable, relaxing, and fun for your teen will promote openness and a sense of security.

4. Be Prepared for Anything

I have had numerous conversations with teens who have shared with me things I'd never have imagined would come out of their mouths. And so, when you make yourself available and your teen begins to see you as one worthy of his or her trust, you might be surprised at how much this precious child of yours may begin to share. So get ready!

5. Ask Questions

If your teen doesn't automatically share, maybe the right way to begin is to ask him or her some questions. Open-ended questions (ones your teen can't answer simply with "yes," "no," or "maybe") are the place to start. For example, if your teen comes home angry or upset over something that happened at school, instead of asking "Do you want to talk about it?" focus on questions that lead to a broader response, such as "What happened today that made you feel this way?"

6. Listen

The most important part of communication is not talking. It is listening. I regularly hear from teens who say that Mom and Dad seldom "listen to what I am really trying to say." I realize some teens use this as an excuse when trying to win a skirmish with Mom and Dad. But sending a clear message to your teen that you are listening, even when you may not agree with the message he or she is sending, could greatly benefit the outcome of the conversation and your relationship.

7. Show That You Are Paying Attention

A teen named Jessica recently e-mailed me this:

> I know my mom loves me. But I don't think she knows how to show it. At least not like she used to. I know she's busy, and I appreciate all she does to take care of my brothers and me. But sometimes I just want to talk about me, my life…my stuff. She's so concerned about her hair, her clothes, and talking on the phone to Stacey (her best friend). Sometimes I wonder who the adult in the relationship really is.

When your teen talks to you, even about what seems trivial, give your full attention. One mom told me how she picks her teen up from school each day. She always turns the phone off so that nothing disrupts their talks. The ride home has proved to be a time for deep conversations.

8. Hit Pause When Necessary

A nine-year-old boy, attending a wedding with his mom, asked, "Why is the bride wearing white?"

His mom replied, "The bride is in white because this is the happiest day of her life."

The boy thought for a moment and then said, "Well, then, why is the groom wearing black?"

Kids can ask questions that leave us perplexed at best. If uncomfortable topics come up in a conversation with your teen, it's okay to hit Pause and take some time to consider your response. Take the matter to prayer, discuss the topic with a spouse, friend, or pastor, and then revisit it with your teen at a later date.

Being a connected parent doesn't mean that you always have all the right answers and advice at a moment's notice. Be honest with your teen by communicating that you need adequate time to consider the topic. Give your teen a time frame within which the two of you will reconvene to continue the conversation. Then stick to your word and approach the subject again after you have taken time to consider the issue.

9. Write Notes

Communication is more than just verbal. One thing I remember most about my years at home is the way my mom wrote me notes and letters. Through the years, she shared poems, scriptures, encouragement, prayers, challenges, and much more. I learned a lot about my mom in her letters—about her character, her virtues, and her desire to make God the priority in her life. Her words provided much more than just the opportunity to communicate to me whatever was on her heart and mind in that moment. These letters also sent me the message that my mom was approachable concerning any issues in life that I faced.

There are times when written communication can allow you the opportunity to express your convictions more clearly and with less inhibition. If it's been some time since you have connected with your teen on a heart level, it could be that a personal note from you would be exactly the kick-start your relationship needs to begin authentic communication.

10. Avoid Avoidance

If you choose, for whatever reason, not to communicate with your teen about a particularly difficult topic, know that you are still sending a message. For instance, topics such as sex, masturbation, homosexuality, and divorce are sometimes treated as taboo in families today. So if you ignore these or other topics, assuming your teen will figure it all out on his or her own, trouble could be right around the corner.

Several years ago I counseled with Michael, a teenage boy contemplating suicide. His desire to end his life was the product of an ongoing struggle with porn that had begun years previously. He shared with me that his father, a pastor, would not discuss the matter with him. The silence from his dad left the son feeling all alone and, as he stated, "confused, dirty, and worthless."

Many teens are hungry for help and guidance. Again, discussing such matters with your teen may be uncomfortable for you at times. But failing to do so could be much more harmful. No matter how inadequate, underprepared, uncomfortable, or uninvolved you may feel, your teen needs to hear from you. If you choose not to communicate with your teen, he or she will "listen" elsewhere for answers.

Keeping the Line Open

Right now, it may appear to you that the last thing your teen wants from you is a conversation. You may have been trying for years to connect and feel as though you have already implemented many of the ideas in this chapter, only to hear silence from the other end. Don't hang up! Keep the line open. Remember, Satan is fighting to deceive you into believing that you are ineffective in communicating with your teen.

It is never too late to begin to communicate. You cannot change what happened in the past, so use that Sweeping Aside Motion. You can only control what you choose to do now. Sure, your teen may not open up to you overnight about every detail of his or her life. But by stepping out in faith, asking questions, and listening, you will have done your part in communicating your desire to be an involved parent. And sometime, even though it may be years from now, you will see the reward of consistently pursuing communication with your teen.

Praying Scripture for Your Teen

Father, You say in Your Word that we are to walk righteously and speak what is right. Help me to do that with my teen. Help my teen to do that with me. Communication is so important. Help my teen and me to talk. Amen.

BASED ON ISAIAH 33:15

7

MEDIA MADNESS

Helping Your Teen Learn to Filter What Comes In

A h, the Bahamas. Imagine you've just arrived at this vacation destination after dreaming about it for years. Sunshine, sand, the ocean, a chair, a good book... Can you picture it? As your toes sink into the sand, the franticness of life back home drifts further and further away.

But suddenly you hear screams. An undercurrent is pulling your teen out to sea, and her feet no longer touch the bottom. With the sound of such cries for help, would you sit by, take another sip of your drink, and slip back into your novel? Of course not! Without even thinking, you would drop everything, race into the water, and fight currents and waves with all you've got to rescue your teen.

Hopefully you'll never experience such a scenario. Yet in many senses your teen *is* being pulled away from the security of your shore by another strong current—an entertainment riptide. And without your help, your teen could drown.

It is critical for me to remind you here that the real enemy is not the world or the culture. "Our struggle is not against flesh and blood, but against the rulers, against the authorities, against the powers of this dark world and against the spiritual forces of evil in the heavenly realms" (Ephesians 6:12).

Remember Jesus's words in John 10:10: "The thief comes only to steal and kill and destroy." Don't be fooled—Jesus makes it clear that the liar and thief is Satan. He fights daily to deceive your teen.

Satan does this in countless ways. One of his most powerful tools is what I call *media madness*. Movies, music, TV, commercials, magazines, the Internet, video games, chat rooms—what madness it can be! The harmful messages being perpetrated by today's media are real and frightening. Above all, these messages are filled with lies.

On mainstream TV, the madness is brought right into your home during prime time. Each year, it seems, this industry tries to push the boundaries further. Today's TV shows offer (and often glamorize) every dirty joke you could possibly dream of, partial nudity, flamboyant pro-homosexual messages, anti-Christian sentiment, and a consistent over-all absence of respect for life, committed relationships, marriage, and God.

Or consider popular teen magazines. Articles and ads send the message to teen girls that how they look is their only ticket to security. Teen boys are told that if they drink the right beer, own expensive cars, and wear the right body spray, women will fall all over them.

Then there is MTV, the big daddy of them all. MTV is the number one channel of choice among twelve- to twenty-five-year-olds. When MTV was birthed in the 1980s, music was the primary objective of the network. Today, though, music is a fraction of the business of MTV. Prevalent on MTV today is a line-up of reality shows that pro-

mote blatant drunkenness during spring break, casual sexual relationships, parties known as "rages," virtual orgies in hot tubs, and just about
anything else you can imagine.

What I find from talking to teens today is that this generation has
become accepting of almost anything, especially when it comes to
morality and spirituality. Even if teens don't take part in immoral acts
or practice alternative religions themselves, the scary truth is that many
don't see anything wrong with these harmful things. When your teen
ingests a steady diet of entertainment that promotes violence, illicit sexual activity, rebellion, hatred, conceit, and other forms of worldly
excess, this spills over into your teen's behavior. It's the old "garbage in,
garbage out" adage at work. Or at the very least, your teen becomes
desensitized to these things.

It's important to understand that what your teen reads, watches,
and listens to is much more than entertainment. This onslaught of
media messages affects how your son or daughter thinks, acts, makes
choices, and ultimately lives life. As adults, we've already formed our
worldviews, but your teen is forming his or her own belief system right
now. Without the maturity or life experience necessary to filter this
madness, he or she needs you. It's your right and responsibility to help
your child recognize this massive deception for what it is.

Parent, please hear this: your real mission is not to hide the world
from your teen; it is to help your teen *filter* the messages of the world
through God-focused lenses.

Isn't this exactly what we see in the ministry of Jesus? Jesus didn't
run from the world. Jesus went to the world. He lived in it, teaching the
world how to see and do life from His perspective.

So, does this mean that you throw caution to the wind and just
hope your teen gets it right at some point? Absolutely not! You can have

tremendous influence over the madness. But this will require that you do your part. You will need a plan, a strategy, a mission. With a little work and creativity, you can become a media-wise parent and teach your teen to discern truth from lies, meaning from madness.

Understanding the Mission

I meet parents who are at their ropes' ends because they believe they have failed miserably at protecting their teens from the madness of the world. One dad told me, "We've failed to protect him from the outside world. I've tried over and again to keep him away from anything that would mislead him or promote impure thoughts in his mind or tempt him. But it hasn't worked."

I appreciate the pain this father is feeling, but I want to point out what I believe is an error in something he said. If parents believe their sole mission is to protect their teens from the outside world, they will always fail. Let me explain.

First, we live in a fallen world. Sin is rampant. So unless you're going to keep your teen under lock and key and hidden away in the basement until he or she is twenty, this approach won't work. The world is waiting, and one day you're going to have to set your teen free.

Second, even if you unplugged the TV, smashed the cell phones, set the computer on fire, destroyed the iPod, and threw out the radio, your teen would still be impacted by the madness. The madness is every-where. Your mission cannot be to keep your teen completely sheltered from the media's influence; this is impossible. Even with the best of intentions, you will fail.

As mentioned above, your real mission is not to hide the world from your teen. It is to help your teen filter the messages of the world through God-focused lenses. Or to put it another way, it's to teach your teen discernment—the ability to distinguish good from evil, to categorize what's helpful and what's harmful, and to make decisions that lead to a life of walking with the Lord.

How do you do that? It's important in this area to hear what teens are saying. When you know what their needs are, you can fight for them in this war.

Welcome to School

Sixteen-year-old Bethany said to me, "I just wish my parents understood this more. I want to download a song or watch a video or whatever, and my dad's first reaction is like, 'No way! Not in my house. We will serve the Lord!' But he doesn't even know what he's criticizing. He just thinks that if I'm not listening to the Gaither band, it's all sin."

Staying aware of this madness isn't an easy task, but it's a necessary one that requires understanding that your teens aren't the only students in the home. Simply stated, to understand the subculture that caters to teens means that you need to become a student of their subculture— it's the Open Book Motion. If you want to know what's truly going on in the world of teens, you must strive to keep up with what's up.

I know what you're thinking: *Jeffrey, I do all I can just to get through the day. And now you're telling me I've got to do more, like surf the Net, watch movies, and read magazines?*

Well, yes and no. No, I am not saying that you must see *every* movie, watch *every* TV show, and know the lyrics to *every* song that your teen does. But yes, you must do more in the sense of not closing yourself off from their world. What if, by just taking a few extra minutes each day, you gained greater insight into the maddening messages competing for your teen's attention—and then helped your teen discern what he or she hears, watches, or downloads?

How might you do that? Let me suggest a few specific ways.

Hello, Teen Vogue

Periodically pick up several teen magazines and read through them. You're not reading them for entertainment; you're reading them to learn about the culture. Read the articles. Look at the advertisements. Get a taste of the worldview being depicted in each. If your teen is up for it, allow him or her to browse through them with you, and then ask your teen some specific questions about a particular article or advertisement and how it aligns (or doesn't align) with Scripture.

Take a Seat

Ask your teen what TV shows he or she watches, then watch those shows together and talk about them. Pay close attention to the language and the show's attitude toward parents, God, dating, sex, and so forth. Or take your teen to a movie of his or her choice, and watch it together with an eye to discernment. Afterward, spend time talking about the show and the spiritual significance, or lack thereof, with your teen.

This exercise will not only show that you care deeply about your teen; it will also help him or her begin to think about cultural messages.

Go Surfing

The next time you are online checking the scores of your favorite team or downloading the recipe for the best chocolate-chip cookies on the planet, go to a search engine and enter such words as "teen Web sites," "teen info," or "teen stuff," and do some research into teen culture. Additionally, check out the many online networking communities available for teens. Ask your teen what his or her favorite online sites are.

By surfing a few teen sites, you'll learn a lot about what your teen is absorbing online.

Hang Out at the Brick-and-Mortar School

A great way to learn what is going on in your teen's life is to volunteer to help with activities or projects at your teen's school. Go, and keep your eyes and ears open. Hear what kids are saying to one another. Notice what they're wearing. Observe how they interact with teachers and other parents. You'll pick up a lot.

Or volunteer to go to a student conference, concert, field trip, mission trip, weekend conference, or summer camp with your teen's class or youth group. Spend a weekend or week with teens, and you're bound to learn a lot...and lose some serious sleep!

Listen to Music You Might Not Like

One of the greatest influences in the life of your teen is music. Listen to the CDs your teen brings home and the songs he or she downloads from the Internet. This will take time on your part. But it is your responsibility as a parent to be aware of the music your teen is pumping into his or her mind and spirit.

A good rule of thumb is to avoid drawing battle lines based on your own musical taste or style. Lyrics, not styles, are important. Go online and research the various bands and artists important to your teen. Find out what the lives of these artists are all about, then sit down and talk with your teen about them. Lead your teen in making wise decisions. You can't control your teen's opinion, but you can illuminate the facts about the music, and you can decide what is and isn't allowed in your home.

Make a Contract

A contract can be a powerful tool for establishing standards and boundaries within the home. I recommend that you make an agreement with your teen for the time he or she is allowed to spend watching TV, playing video games, and listening to music and for the content that is acceptable. Designate a specific and reasonable amount of time each day or week that you will allow your teen to engage in these activities. Any media restrictions you have established need to be documented in your agreement. Give your teen a hand in creating the document, then have your teen sign the document at the bottom.

What's feasible in a contract? Well, it depends on your home, your teen, and your temperament. A contract might stipulate issues surrounding the following.

Length of time. "You are allowed to watch TV each school night *or* play video games for a total of two hours (three hours per day on weekends). You are allowed to watch two movies per week. You are allowed to be online up to 10 p.m."

Content. "You are allowed to watch G- and PG-rated movies. PG-13- and R-rated movies are generally not allowed, but we may make certain exceptions if you discuss the movie with us first (for example, *The Passion of the Christ* and *Schindler's List* were both rated R but may be worth watching). You are allowed to play video games from a list that we as parents have preapproved."

Creating a contract that really works requires that you be creative in how you design it, flexible in how you implement it (if something isn't working, you may need to revise the contract), and faithful in making sure your teen adheres to its stipulations, with negative consequences built in (that is, a privilege is removed if the contract is not kept). Remember, the battle is a marathon, not a sprint. Use your Deep Breath Posture, and run the race well.

Become My Friend

Join the Jeffrey Dean Ministries mailing list. Our ministry produces a newsletter for those eighteen and older that focuses on teen culture. It's called the *E3 Update*. Visit our Web site, JeffreyDean.com, for more information.

Create a Family Mission Statement

When it comes to navigating the media madness, I find that one of the most helpful tools is developing a family mission statement.

Give each family member time to write down issues and ideas that are important to him or her and pertinent to this topic. Then come together as a family to develop a family mission statement with which each family member agrees. Select a scripture to be a part of this statement. Use your mission statement as a guide to help you handle issues, dilemmas, and arguments both at home and away from home. When facing a family crisis, strive to make sure the result is in alignment with the family mission statement. Check out what Sherie and Steve told me:

> We attended your parenting conference several months ago and just wanted you to know the difference it has made in our home since we applied the techniques you suggested. At first, I'll be honest, we were a little skeptical. Our oldest is sixteen, and he is pretty set in his ways. But we were determined, as you encouraged, to do our part.
>
> The first night of our family devo time, we asked each of our three children to write a mission statement that each would like the family to follow. The next week, we gave each of them time to read his or her statement. It was eye-opening for us to listen to the requests and obvious needs of our children both

emotionally and physically. As we have made it a priority to spend even more time talking together as a family, we realize that our kids do want more of us. Thank you for laying it out there for us and pushing us as parents to do more.

Equipping Your Teen to Pursue God

Teens need to be challenged to pursue God and defend their faith when under the influence of the media madness. Since you are the number one influence in your teen's life, your teen will be more likely to embrace this challenge if you embrace it and demonstrate it in the home. When you defend your own faith and articulate your own worldview, you are equipping your teen to do the same.

Remember, the secret to winning this spiritual war is not just avoiding worldliness and sin, though we are certainly called to do that. The only way we can win so fierce a war is to passionately pursue God, press into Him, and delight in Him. This is partially covered in the chapter about dreaming big for your teen. I also talk about this in more depth in chapter 15, "Going Public with God."

The media madness tells us that everything *else* will satisfy us, but as Christians, we know that everything else *but God* will leave us used up and empty. If you can help your teen understand this fact, you will be handing him or her the secret to the purpose of life. *You* know what the world doesn't know: we exist to know God, to enjoy Him, and to glorify Him. It's wonderfully uncomplicated. Pass this truth on to your child.

You may be feeling frightened of all the negative influences to which your teen is continually being exposed. Don't be. Yes, the dangers are real, and the results can be devastating if your teen gets sucked into the lies. However, learning about teen culture, continuing to address these issues with your teen, and living as a godly example will help your teen develop a worldview in tune with God's desires.

Praying Scripture for Your Teen

Father, I kneel before You and pray that out of Your glorious riches You may strengthen my teen with power through Your Spirit in my teen's inner being, so that Christ may dwell in my teen's heart through faith. And I pray that my teen, being rooted and established in love, may have power to grasp how wide and long and high and deep is the love of Christ, and to know this love that surpasses knowledge—that my teen may be filled to the measure of all the fullness of God. Amen.

BASED ON EPHESIANS 3:14–19

8

ANYTHING GOES ON THE INTERNET

Helping Your Teen Honor God Online

The Internet has become as much a part of life today as eating, sleeping, and talking on cell phones. The Web is having a tremendous impact upon today's family. For better or worse, it is here to stay.

Obviously there are many benefits to the Internet, such as countless educational opportunities, up-to-the minute news, live video conferencing, research, communication, and more. But there are just as many dangers. As a parent, you need to understand these dangers and develop a strategy to ensure that your teen develops healthy surfing habits.

It's true that most of today's teens are ahead of most parents in both understanding the technology and being comfortable using it. Some teens even build a lifestyle around the Internet and have—if they want it—the ability to keep their parents in the dark about what they're up to. So I want to acknowledge up-front what you may be feeling when it comes to this area: outmanned, mystified, even intimidated.

I won't pretend to have all the answers in this area, but I will tell you that there is hope. Part of the response will be your relationship with your teen and the communication habit you have with him or her. Trust and talking are excellent places to start.

It takes more than that, though. As I said, in this battle the Internet is both an opportunity and a liability. So our challenge is twofold: to help our teens learn to use the good and to protect our teens from the bad.

Truths About the Internet

Are you ready to use your Open Book Motion and become a student of teen culture when it comes to the online world? Walk with me through six specific characteristics and challenges of the Internet revolution. In this world, knowledge is power. Did you know that...?

1. People Can Be "Cooler" Online

I recently heard a comedy song about a guy who described himself as a loser in real life. Yet online he was cooler than cool. Offline, his social life consisted of watching *Jeopardy!* with his roommates, but every time he jumped online, he transformed into a party animal.

Sadly, the humor in this song fades in comparison with the reality. One of the attractions—and one of the great alarms—of the Net is anonymity. Anyone can become someone else when online.

Anonymity breeds danger. When visiting a chat room, visiting a social-networking site, or simply answering a random e-mail, your teen does not necessarily know with whom he or she is communicating.

2. It's More Like "TeenLiar.com"

The World *Wild* Web, as I like to call it, is the leading source of information for most teens today. But it's also a prime source for *mis-*

information, lies, predators, and harmful content that clearly contradicts God's truth.

It would be impossible for me to list every site online that may be sending your teen inaccurate, misleading, or unbiblical information. But as an example, I want to bring to your attention one of the hottest Web sites visited by teens today: www.teenliar.com. Whoops, wait a minute—its URL is actually www.teenwire.com.

This Web site is owned and operated by an organization that is an outspoken advocate for abortion, homosexuality, and premarital sex. It speaks the language of teens and tells them what they want to hear in a way that seems nonthreatening, inviting, and often consequence free. The organization that produces this site perpetuates the myth that it is the "expert" on all things sexual. Cool graphics, teen jargon, and interactive diagrams of the female and male anatomy that look more like porn than medically accurate depictions of the body are just a part of the darkness of Teenwire.com.

Recently I read an article at Teenwire.com dealing with homosexuality and why it's "a good thing" to "come out." This Web site won't give me permission to reprint the article here, but if you want a copy of it, try looking it up or go to JeffreyDean.com and click on "contact JD" to send me an e-mail; our office will make sure you get a copy. This is sick stuff filling the heads of our nation's teens. I also found several articles on this same site encouraging sex play and homosexual experimentation.

Here is an opportunity for you to exercise your commitment to be a student of the culture. If you want to know what thousands of teens across the country are downloading at Teenwire.com every day, take some time to visit this site. Let me warn you, though: some of what you will find there is disturbing.

3. It's All Out There (and I Do Mean All)

Beyond Teenwire.com, there are plenty of additional harmful Web sites for teens out there. I wish I had space to list them all. Unfortunately, once a teen logs on to many of these "for teens only" sites, he or she is bombarded with spam and e-blasts encouraging the teen viewer to continue returning for more.

On one teen site I visited, I was amazed to find an article dealing with the topic of abstinence that drew a line between what this site described as "periodic abstinence" and "continuous abstinence." According to the site, periodic abstinence means that a teen girl says no to sex only on her days of possibly getting pregnant. The next paragraph explained that continuous abstinence is usually the best choice. But the article was clearly muddying this subject. Several articles on this same site offered detailed steps on how to give oral sex, how to masturbate alone or with a partner, and how to split a condom so that you can use it to give oral sex to a girl while using protection. This same site calls abortion "a very safe procedure" and mentions on several occasions that a second abortion is "no big deal."

One of the obvious red flags to this and many sites geared to teens is the "do not disturb" attitude toward parents who wish to keep tabs on what their teens can find at this site. One teen site I often visit has this disclaimer for parents who visit the site: "This Web site is for teens. This is their place."

Pardon me, Mr. Web Site Provider, but these are not *your* teens you are hurting with your Web site. Parents have a right to know what you're trying to shove down teens' throats.

These are just a few examples of the dangers on the World Wild Web. Though the Internet may not be of interest to you, it most likely is to your teen. It is here to stay. And so are its dangers.

4. Your Teen Probably Visits at Least One SNS

Have you heard of SNS's (social-networking sites)? Chances are, your teen has visited one, along with the tens of millions of others who visit and navigate through SNS's each day. Right now, the three most popular SNS's for teens seem to be Facebook, MySpace, and Xanga. (Their popularity can change quickly.) There are more than five hundred SNS's up and running right now. For a complete list, log on to Wikipedia.org and type in "List of social networking websites."

An SNS is an online place where a user creates a profile and builds a personal network that connects him or her to other users. In the past five years, such sites have rocketed from a niche activity into a phenomenon. Most every teen I know uses one or more social-networking sites.

As the Internet grows and the number of users increases, more people will have access to your teen's personal information. You may be aware that social-networking sites allow users to join communities and thus become your teen's "friend." On the surface, this idea seems innocent. But SNS's also have what is known as the "friends of friends" equation. By providing information about themselves and by using blogs, chat rooms, e-mail, or instant messaging, users can communicate within a limited community or with the world at large.

While these sites can increase your teen's circle of friends, they also can increase your teen's exposure to people with less-than-friendly intentions. This is where you must be ready to fight for your teen. Fighting, in this case, means establishing smart surfing guidelines when it comes to the online social scene your teen frequents.

Some SNS's, such as MySpace, prohibit anyone under fourteen years of age from using their Web site. (Xanga and Facebook require users to be thirteen or older.) But this does not prohibit kids younger than fourteen from lying about their ages and establishing personal profiles.

MySpace has developed special software to review the profiles of its members in an effort to catch underage members. But it is not entirely childproof.

If you are wondering whether your underage teen (or teen of any age) has established a social site on an SNS that prohibits underage users, here are a few suggestions:

- Try the direct approach: ask your teen if he or she has a profile on an SNS.
- Search MySpace.com or other SNS's using your teen's e-mail address, name, or school, or other points of interest about your teen.
- If your teen does have a profile, check it out, even if you have to join (or create a profile) to gain access. You might be surprised at what you learn about your teen.
- Decide what you will do from here. If your teen is under fourteen, the profile needs to be removed.
- Ask your teen to remove it. MySpace has information on how to remove a profile.
- Use this as an opportunity to communicate with your teen about the importance of being a person of integrity and honesty. Ask such questions as "Why did you create a profile?" "Why didn't you ask me first?" "Do you think it is okay to have a profile at MySpace even though you are underage?"
- Explain the dangers that exist online.

Here is another opportunity to keep the lines of communication open with your young teen. Helping your teen establish trust in your wisdom can help both of you develop an open and honest relationship that will continue throughout the teen years.

5. Online, It's "Tell Me What I Want to Hear"

The first confirmed death in the United States by an Internet sexual predator was in 2002. The victim was a thirteen-year-old girl. She was popular, made good grades, and was a cheerleading co-captain at her private Catholic school. But she met a guy online and eventually met him in person. He killed her. This tragic story is a horrific reminder to all parents of the fight we are in to protect our teens from the darkness of this world.

Porn is huge on the Internet (we'll discuss this in detail in chapter 9), but it is not the only online enemy. The threat of sexual predators lurking a click away and propositioning your teen is real.

While speaking at a church several years ago, I was saddened to learn that the pastor's daughter had been assaulted after agreeing to meet a person she had met in an online chat room. After several months of chatting online with someone she thought was a seventeen-year-old boy from a neighboring city, she was lured into meeting this cyber-predator at a local gas station. He turned out to be thirty-six. She was abducted and raped repeatedly before being released. After this horrific ordeal, this young girl told authorities she had gone to the gas station because the man had told her things that she always wanted to hear from a guy.

These cases are extreme. But it is critical that you remain alert and aware of the dangers awaiting your teen online. I find that most victims of sexual predators online are teens considered to be loners. They often feel insecure, are looking for love, and so get conned into a meeting. Most teens believe they are communicating with someone similar in age. Almost always, as in the case of the pastor's daughter I mentioned, they are told exactly want they want to hear.

There are several warning signs that your teen is dancing with danger online. Ask yourself questions like these:

- *How much time does my teen spend online?* With ubiquitous cell phones (which have Internet access) and with the laptops that many high-school students carry to and from school these days, it's hard to discern this by mere observation. Your teen may be online far more than you think. Maybe your answer is, "I have no idea how much time my teen spends online." If so, then it may be that your teen is in a dangerous place.

- *Does my teen have a lot of friends, or is he or she more of a loner?* Teens who don't have a large circle of friends can be easier targets for sexual predators.

- *Is my teen a risk taker?* Teens can use the Internet to engage in risky behavior or post messages on blogs or profiles suggesting interest in promiscuous behavior.

- *Is my teen sheltered?* Surprisingly, a sheltered teen, especially a girl, could be easier prey if a predator promises her gifts, jewelry, his love, marriage, and more. I find that teens who have been more sheltered than others often have a lower skepticism threshold. They have never had to mistrust anybody, so it's not something they readily do.

- *Does my teen keep me informed about his or her surfing habits? Does my teen quickly exit a page or make the screen go dark when someone enters the room?* If so, he or she could be hiding something you need to be aware of.

- *Does my teen have a MySpace, Xanga, or Facebook page?* If so, ask questions about it, such as "Who are your online friends?" and "Do you have privacy settings to block others from viewing your profile or entering your page?"

- *Do I know my teen's favorite sites?* If not, you had better find out.

- *Does my teen IM (instant message)?* If so, who is on his or her buddy list? Where did these names come from? It is a good idea to go through your teen's list with him or her and have your teen tell you the real name of everyone on the list and how your teen knows each one.

- *Does my teen have his or her own blog or Web site?* If so, check the site out. What information does your teen give out about himself or herself, friends, family, and so on? What pictures are posted? Does your teen show a side of his or her personality you've never seen before?

These are just a few suggestions for you to consider pertaining to your teen's surfing habits. Keep in mind that although your teen has a right to privacy, you still have a right to know about the life your teen leads online.

Frequently review the above list, asking questions and researching your teen's online habits. Watch for any change in behavior. Is your teen acting differently? Has he or she changed friends lately? Is he or she receiving phone calls from someone you don't know or from numbers you do not recognize?

All of this information can seem overwhelming, especially if you have not implemented such rigid practices in the past. And admittedly, this is work. But it is worth it for the safety of your teen.

6. Cookies Are Not Always Good

Your teen can visit a site, go into a chat room, or enter personal information for various reasons, such as to register for a giveaway, and unknowingly leave more information than intended. This happens through what are called *cookies*. Cookies gather information that a person supplies voluntarily while online. By entering his or her name, address, phone number, or e-mail address, your teen is supplying personal data that many companies will pay to obtain.

Cookies can result in your teen getting exposed to e-mails and pop-up windows trying to sell just about anything under the sun. This is a major annoyance. It also means that information about your teen could become available to someone who would want to hurt him or her. This is why it is vital that you and your family establish safeguards now.

Safeguarding Your Teen

What's one of the best ways to safeguard your family? Set up a safe surfing system. This is an agreement that family members sign for safe Internet use. If your teen or any child in your family, regardless of age, spends time online, these principles will be helpful to you in establishing healthy online habits for your family. Don't buy Satan's lie that this is unnecessary for your family or that your teen is immune to the dangers of the Net. Buying such a lie and choosing to do nothing could be harmful to your family.

Keep in mind that some of these principles may be more beneficial to your family than others, depending on the age of your teen. The important thing is to establish a safe surfing system, clearly articulate the system to your teen, and then live by it when surfing. Your safe surfing system might look something like this:

We agree to…
1. Never fill out questionnaires or any forms online or give out personal information (name, address,

phone, Social Security number, school we attend, names of friends, etc.) about ourselves or anyone else to anyone we meet online without Mom/Dad's approval.

2. Never give out any password to anyone we meet online, even to our friends.

3. Never agree to meet in person with someone whom we have met online without Mom/Dad's approval and presence.

4. Never enter a chat room without being knowledgeable about it. We will remember that some "friends" we meet online who say they are teens may not actually be teens.

5. Never respond to an e-mail, instant message, or chat room comment that makes us feel uncomfortable or unsafe. In fact, we will never respond to an unknown sender, period. When encountering such a situation, we will leave the chat room immediately, or ignore the one who sent the e-mail, and communicate the situation to Mom/Dad. We commit to tell Mom/Dad about anything happening online that causes us concern, fear, or anger or seems odd.

6. Never discuss with anyone online personal information about our jobs, including where, when, and at what time(s) we work.

7. Never respond to or send an e-mail to someone we meet online without the permission of Mom/Dad.

8. Never send a picture over the Internet or via regular mail to anyone we meet online.

9. Never buy or order products online or give out any credit-card information online without Mom/Dad's permission.

10. Never let our friends have use of our computer without the approval of Mom/Dad.

Signed _____ (all kids in family)

www.DoYourPartNow.com

Your safe surfing system is a crucial part of your attempts to safeguard your teen online. But you can't leave it at that. There's more you can and should do to minimize the possibility of your teen's surfing in dangerous waters. Below are the top steps to take today.

Understand Your Teen's Vulnerability

Recently I spoke at a church where one mom approached me to say, "My daughter spends hours and hours online. If she's not in school and not eating or sleeping, she's probably online. It's like she's dating her computer."

Teens (and adults) can quickly become consumed with the Internet. If you are not careful, you can allow your teen to develop a relationship with the Internet. Surfing the Net can quickly become a replacement for real-world communication in the life of your teen. Your teen needs to learn not to rely on a computer for companionship. And he or she needs your help to do this.

Often, the most vulnerable teens are those who struggle with low self-esteem and identity issues. The computer will never disagree with your teen, talk back, or start a fight. Likewise, your teen can meet a person online who seems to fulfill every need he or she is feeling. Your teen can quickly develop trust in an online relationship with someone he or she does not fully know.

Place the Computer in a High-Traffic Area

Under no circumstance should your teen have a computer with Internet access in his or her bedroom. This is particularly true for teen boys. Teens tell me that the number one place they check out porn is behind closed doors at home. It is essential that you place the computer in a high-traffic area in your home, such as a family room.

Limit Your Teen's Use of the Internet

Similar to setting a Friday-night curfew or setting boundaries on appropriate phone use, you need to apply family rules to time spent surfing and chatting online. Sit down with your teen and discuss the reasons why you are establishing time limits on surfing.

Use a Filter

There are many good filters available to screen out inappropriate Internet sites. With a little research on your part (for example, pull up Google and type in "Christian Internet filtering"), you can find a filter that will protect your teen from many (though not all) of the inappropriate sites online. Filters are not perfect, but they are a big step in the right direction.

You may also want to consider using what is called a *closed secure system*. Unlike filters or blocking software, with a closed secure system your teen will be denied access to any site that you have not preselected as an appropriate site for your teen to visit. Many of these systems also provide features to block e-mail and chat-room access—the methods often used by sexual predators.

Check Your Computer's History

Periodically check the history of your Internet browser to see what sites have been viewed on your computer. This is something every computer allows you to do.

Below is information on how to check computer history in two different ways. If one of these processes does not work for the browser you use, the steps to checking your history should be similar to one of the processes below. If you have any remaining questions about checking your Internet browser, you can contact your Internet service provider (ISP), and they should be able to walk you through the necessary steps.

- For PC users using Internet Explorer, click on Start > All Programs > Internet Explorer > Temporary Internet Files.
- For Macintosh users, click on Menu > Windows > History.

After attending one of our Plugged-in Parenting events, one father e-mailed me to say that he went home that night to check the history of recent online activity on their computer. He said, "There was no history. It was all gone. I knew immediately that someone was trying to hide something. So we had a family meeting to get to the bottom of it!"

This father found out something you need to know: history can be easily erased. So if you really want to keep tabs on your teen's surfing habits, know that there is software available that will send you reports detailing every Web site visited by your teen. If your son or daughter has struggled in the past with Internet porn, this is an excellent accountability tool.

Let your teen know that you will consistently be checking to see where he or she has surfed. Remember, periodically checking up on your teen does not make you a nag or secretive parent. It makes you a good parent. It is also good to occasionally check to see who your teen has been e-mailing and who has been e-mailing your teen.

Take Extreme Measures When Necessary

If you believe your teen is hiding something from you concerning activity online, then you need to do something *now*. And as a parent, you must be willing to take extreme measures when necessary to protect your teen. For example, your teen needs to understand that the use of the computer is a privilege that can be taken away.

Communicate

Most of all, keep communication lines open. Ask questions. Make it clear to your teen that you will remain proactive in communicating with him or her about surfing habits. And remember, it is never too late to begin to communicate.

Surfing with Integrity

As always, my goal is to help you point your teen back to Scripture. Matthew 10:16 says, "I am sending you out like sheep among wolves. Therefore be as shrewd as snakes and as innocent as doves."

Encourage your teen to make this verse his or her surfing scripture. The likelihood of your teen's falling prey to a sexual predator may be minimal. But this chapter is about far more than simply helping your teen avoid a tragedy. The greater message is to encourage your teen to live a life that honors God, particularly while surfing the Net.

No one may ever fully know what your teen is doing online. But the simple truth is that your teen's online life is either honoring to God or dishonoring to God. Everything your teen says, shows, types, and posts online lets the world know who your teen lives for. Work to instill in your teen an online lifestyle that proclaims, "I am a follower of Christ."

Praying Scripture for Your Teen

Lord, cyberspace is a wonderful and terrible place. Help me to teach my teen how to be shrewd in avoiding danger online while remaining innocent and holy. Help us always to honor You with our use of the Internet. Amen.

BASED ON MATTHEW 10:16

9

UNPLUGGING PORNOGRAPHY

Helping Your Teen Escape the Trap

Dear Jeffrey,

   Thanks for coming to Ichthus Festival again. Man, I love hearing you speak. I want to thank you for letting me come clean with you about my past. I still feel guilty a lot about all the stuff I've done. Like I said then, I'm the last person anyone would have guessed would be so deep into that junk [porn]. And you're right. I can still remember so many of those pictures, even though it's been months since I looked at porn. I'm gonna keep doing everything you told me to do. Thanks for letting me talk about it all and for just listening.

   Name withheld

I get notes like this all the time. What's encouraging is that the teens who write them are taking some strides in the right direction. What's sad is that many teens are caught in the deadly snare of pornography and haven't taken the first step toward freedom.

Pornography is everywhere. Statistics leave our heads spinning about how many pornographic sites are on the Web today, how many new porn sites go live every day, and how huge, powerful, and pervasive the pornographic video industry is. The revenue of the pornography industry is larger than the revenues of the top technology companies combined: Microsoft, Google, Amazon, eBay, Yahoo!, Apple, Netflix, and EarthLink.[1] And porn is only a click away. If you want it, you can find it quicker than quick. Even when you are not looking for it, porn can still find you. And once you've downloaded it into your mind's hard drive, the harmful images can keep replaying over and over again.

Based on the widespread availability of pornography today, one might conclude that we as a society are increasingly accepting its presence as normal. And as a matter of fact, for some people, porn seems to be no big deal. For instance, The Barna Group reported that 29 percent of all born-again adults in the United States believe it is morally acceptable to view movies depicting explicit sexual behavior.[2]

I'd say these people are not facing the fact that porn is dangerous to the core. It sucks every bit of truth, contentment, honesty, character, loyalty, and reality out of the mind and soul of the one plugging into it. Porn leaves people feeling hopeless, guilty, and ashamed. I know what I'm talking about. I communicate on a regular basis with teens who struggle with addiction to porn. And these are not oddball, sadistic, perverted teens but everyday, honor-roll, churchgoing, love-their-parents, striving-to-live-for-Jesus teens.

---

1. "Pornography Statistics," Family Safe Media, www.familysafemedia.com/pornography_statistics.html (accessed June 17, 2008).
2. "Statistics on Pornography, Sexual Addiction and Online Perpetrators," Safe Families, www.safefamilies.org/sfStats.php (accessed June 17, 2008).

Who is hurt by pornography? While we often think of the porn industry as targeting only males, a recent study showed that the industry is targeting females as well. About one in three visitors to adult Web sites is female.[3] That means your daughter is at risk just as your son is.

No teen today is immune to the possibility of falling into the trap of porn. It can happen quickly. It can happen unintentionally. It can happen to *your* teen. One study showed that a whopping 90 percent of all eight- to sixteen-year-olds had viewed pornography online—most inadvertently while doing homework.[4]

I often meet adults who can't fathom how someone could get caught up in such filth as pornography. Even when some parents realize their son or daughter is addicted to porn, the Enemy has often won the fight by convincing them that they are helpless and ill equipped to help their teen.

But the struggle with pornography isn't different from the struggle with any other sin: Satan presents us with a dangerous, cleverly packaged lie that looks inviting. We are tempted. And temptation gives birth to sin.

Sin affects us all (see Romans 3:23). What sins are evident in your life? If your teen struggles with porn, let him know that he is not alone and that you understand the struggle, because you struggle with your own sins. Maybe you have even struggled with the specific sin of porn viewing, and therefore you can share in a very personal way what that struggle has been like and how you have achieved victory.

3. Jerry Ropelato, "Internet Pornography Statistics," Top Ten Reviews, http://internet-filter-review.toptenreviews.com/internet-pornography-statistics.html (accessed June 17, 2008).

4. David C. Bissette, "Internet Pornography Statistics: 2003," HealthyMind.com, http://healthymind.com/s-porn-stats.html (accessed June 17, 2008).

Certainly we cannot be passive about the problem of pornography. Hebrews 12:1 tells us to "throw off everything that hinders and the sin that so easily entangles." So, parent, it's time to act. It's time to arm yourself with the necessary tools to wage this war alongside your teen. Are you ready for this battle? It starts with learning more about what you're up against.

How Porn Finds Your Teen

This is a problem: if your teen is online, porn will find him or her. For instance, a sophomore in college whom I met on the road last year told me that he had gotten hooked on Internet porn while in high school. During his senior year, he was required to write a term paper on human anatomy for an advanced-placement biology class. One afternoon he was routinely surfing the Web, reading about the study of the human body. Innocently clicking on a link in search of images of the female anatomy, he suddenly saw a porn site appear. He quickly left the site. But the more he sat in front of his computer, the more he thought about those images. Several minutes later, he found himself going back to check them out again…and again. Thus began a dark journey that lasted most of his senior year of high school.

One click. That's all it takes.

I've had countless teens tell me that they have received inappropriate spam mail—unsolicited, commercial e-mail that often leads to a Web site, usually pornographic. Sometimes the initial spam messages appear innocuous, such as an invitation to check out a magazine subscription or some cartoons or jokes. Sometimes the advertisements are a bit racier.

I got one of these just yesterday on my cell phone. It said, "Hey, sexy, I saw your profile online and want to send you a few pics of me. Click this link below and let's get to know each other."

Whoever sent this spam got my e-mail address from somewhere. It may have been from a program that crawls the Web, searching for e-mail addresses. Or my address may have been sold to a company. Or it may have been from a program that searches for names on the Internet and randomly creates plausible e-mail addresses from the original name, hoping that one in a thousand will hit the mark.

Pornography is aggressive. Pornography seeks and destroys. It's imperative that you know about the fight you are in against pornography.

The Trouble with Porn

What's so harmful about looking at pornography? Isn't it just a phase that all teens go through, particularly boys?

Nothing could be further from the truth.

As your teen begins to look at porn consistently, his or her view of the opposite sex will change. Eventually your teen will stop seeing people as God sees them and begin seeing them merely as a means by which desires can be fulfilled. Pornography turns other people into objects of lust.

If your teen dates, typically it will only be a matter of time before he or she becomes more physical with the dating partner. The fantasy world being downloaded into his or her mind will fight to turn itself into reality by encouraging your teen to use people to fulfill personal lusts. And as your son or daughter tries to act out the sexual behaviors seen online, the perceived need for self-gratification will damage not only your teen's relationships during the dating years but also his or her relationship with a future mate.

Furthermore, as your teen dives deeper into the world of porn, his or her character will begin to be eroded, even destroyed. This isn't my idea. Galatians 6:7–8 says, "A man reaps what he sows. The one who sows to please his sinful nature, from that nature will reap destruction." Teens are being greatly fooled if they believe they can casually check out porn and still live the lives God would have them live. If your son or daughter sows to please lust, destruction is soon to follow.

Dishonesty within this area of life will spill over into other areas of your teen's life. Basically, as your teen gives Satan one area of life, it will only be a matter of time before the Enemy pursues and demands other areas as well.

What You Can Do

If your teen is into porn, you don't have time to waste. With every look and every image, your teen is going deeper and deeper into darkness. The Enemy wants you to feel guilty. He wants you to question how this could have happened to your teen. He will work overtime to convince you that you have failed miserably. He wants to knock you down in the first round so you will crawl back to your corner, give up, and be defeated before you even decide to fight.

But Satan is a liar. Regardless of what has transpired to get you to this point, this battle can be won. Your teen doesn't have to continue down this degrading path. First John 4:4 says, "My dear children, you come from God and belong to God. You have already won a big victory over those false teachers, for the Spirit in you is far stronger than anything in the world" (MSG). The One in you is greater than the deceiver in this world, and God can bring your son or daughter out of this place of darkness.

I have yet to counsel a teen struggling with porn who desired to continue struggling. Nobody wants to be enslaved to sin and remain on the road to destruction. Yet many who desire to escape from the bondage in which they are living have little knowledge of how to overcome its grip.

If your teen is struggling with porn, he or she will need your help. Here are eight vital steps to help your teen find freedom from the darkness.

1. Get to the Facts

It is essential that you talk with your teen about porn. If you don't, who will?

Many parents talk about porn and sexuality with their teen but do it only indirectly. I say, don't dance around the issue. Get right to the point. Be specific. Share with your teen the effects porn will have on his or her life.

Even if you do not suspect your teen is involved in porn, don't wait to have such a talk. Remember, if your teen spends time online, it is inevitable that at some point he or she will be exposed to the raw, filthy, multibillion-dollar-a-year business of porn. If you have caught your teen in the act, at first your teen may deny that the struggle exists or try to minimize its effects on his or her life. It is critical that you explain to your teen that Satan is out to get him or her hooked. What an awesome moment this can be to strengthen your relationship with your teen and help your teen see you as someone who longs to protect him or her from harm!

2. Love the Teen; Hate the Sin

As you implement each of the following steps in your fight to defeat this darkness in your teen's life, you will need to constantly remind your son or daughter that your love has not and will not change. Your teen needs to know that, though you disagree with his or her actions, your ultimate desire is to help your child defeat this addiction and be restored to a pure life. Every day, communicate to your teen that the sin is the thing you hate, not your teen.

3. Realize That a Promise Isn't Enough

When your teen has been caught in the act, his or her first response may be to quickly apologize, plead for your forgiveness, and promise to never do it again. And yet, though your teen's desire to repent may be genuine, it may be only a matter of time before the addiction wins him or her over again.

For a teen struggling with porn, a promise to change isn't enough. You need to help your teen make the promise a reality.

4. Encourage Confession and Submission

Your son or daughter's involvement in the world of sex, lies, and porn may be a shock to you. But it is not to God. God is aware of every filthy image that has ever been downloaded into your teen's mind. And the best part is that He still loves your teen.

Jeremiah 29:11 tells us that the Lord has a plan for each of us, a plan to prosper us and to give us hope and a future. The future of this plan often begins with confession (see 1 John 1:9). Lead your teen through a time of confession with God. Encourage your teen to be completely honest with God as he or she confesses mistakes and receives God's forgiveness.

Your teen not only needs your consistent involvement, support, and accountability, but he or she also must be willing to submit future choices, actions, and thoughts to God. This could mean that for a while your teen commits to completely avoiding any access to the computer, Internet, TV, or movies, and any form of entertainment that may tempt him or her to check out porn again.

God desires to be in complete control of your teen's life. This can happen only as your teen chooses to submit to God each day. Temptation will be a daily battle for your teen. And so daily submission to God is the key to winning the battle.

Of course, you also have to take some practical steps to protect your teen from porn.

5. Take Inventory and Destroy

Consider the types of media outlets your teen has access to in the home: movies, satellite and cable TV, videos, music, the Internet. Consider what your teen watches and listens to. What influences do these media messages have, or have the potential to have, on your teen?

If you suspect or know that your teen is struggling with porn, remove the source from the home immediately. If this is a computer, make sure its location is in a high-traffic area in the home and that your teen never has access to it unless in your presence. If the source is a TV, it must go. If the source is magazines, they must go. No questions, no rationalizing—whatever it is, it must go!

This sounds strong, but remember, this is war. You cannot expect to defeat the enemy if the enemy still has access to your home. Of course, this purging of your home will not eliminate access to all the porn in the world. But by removing the immediate sources, you will be sending a strong message to your teen that you are prepared to take extreme measures to break the bondage in which he or she is living.

6. Develop a Strategy for the Future

It is unrealistic to think that just because you remove sources of temptation from the home, your teen will never again be tempted to use porn. So it's important for you to develop a strategy for your teen, while both inside and outside the home, to help him or her avoid repeating an addictive behavior.

Because each teen's situation, lifestyle, and personality is unique, there is no one strategy that will work for everyone. I recommend that you take some time with your spouse (if married) and outline a game plan before discussing it with your teen. That game plan should include, but not be limited to, the following:

Establishing a routine. Your teen needs to see the importance of a disciplined, routine schedule. The key here is not to isolate your teen from his daily activities, hobbies, and interests completely. But setting boundaries on what he or she can do will help your teen develop a greater sense of security.

Work to help your teen's schedule stay full enough so that his or her mind remains occupied. Chores, sports, a part-time job, volunteering, and more can be helpful outlets.

Approving friendships. One teen told me that his mom and dad found out he was checking out porn at home, so they removed the computer from his room. Then he started checking it out at his best friend's house.

Remember, your teen's friends play a huge role in his or her decision making. Choosing friends who are in line with God's will for your teen's life is a critical step to overcoming the temptations to check out porn. First Corinthians 15:33 says, "Bad company corrupts good character." It is essential that your teen choose friends that push him or her toward God rather than ones that pull him or her away. Let your teen know that you will have debriefings about who your teen's friends are and where he or she spends time.

There's much more on this important topic of friendships to come in a later chapter.

Killing the lies. Satan often wins the porn war when he wins the war in your teen's mind. Communicate to your teen that Satan will work to sell him or her such lies as these:

- "What's the big deal? It's just a naked picture. Besides, looking at porn is a lot better than sleeping with someone."
- "I'm so good in every other area of life. This is just my one issue."
- "No one is going to know. And what harm will really come from it?"
- "I deserve this. I've had a really tough week."

Communicating with your teen. If your teen has been checking out porn for some time, then it is highly probable that he or she will experience setbacks in separating from this darkness. The evil forces will pull out all their weapons to try to drive harmful desires deeper into your teen's mind. The best way to control these moments is to have consistent times of communication with your teen. Regularly ask questions such as these:

- "How are you feeling about your struggle?"
- "Have you had any setbacks?"
- "What's going on in your head?"

Let your teen see that you are serious about fighting with him or her against the Enemy in this area, no matter how long it takes.

Establishing goals. Develop a set of goals your teen strives to achieve. As he or she proves trustworthy, the teen will then be granted more freedom. Use this as an encouragement to help your teen see progress.

7. Get Your Teen into the Word

A key to killing the addiction to porn in the heart and mind of your teen rests in the teen's own commitment to consistently spend time in God's Word.

Help your teen find Scripture verses to memorize, carry in his or her wallet, or hang on a mirror or locker that will help your teen in a crisis moment. Relying on Scripture when faced with a temptation is exactly what Jesus did when He was tempted (see Matthew 4).

Continually encourage your teen to spend time with God, praying and reading the Bible.

8. Pray Like Crazy

The greatest strategy that you can implement to protect your teen from Satan's lies about pornography (and everything else the Enemy throws at him or her) is prayer.

Prayer is your source of strength when the fight takes you into the eleventh round. Prayer is your greatest weapon against Satan's ploys to get your teen to take a bite of the forbidden fruit. Prayer is the greatest "kaboom" you have against the Enemy. I don't call prayer the Ultimate Power Stance for nothing.

—

Applying these eight strategies may not be comfortable for either you or your teen. But this battle is not about comfort. It's about fighting an enemy whose goal is to steal, kill, and destroy. The fight isn't always easy. But God is on your side. You are never fighting alone!

Praying Scripture for Your Teen

God, just like Job said, I pray that my teen and I would both make a covenant with our eyes not to look lustfully at anyone. I pray that we would abstain from sinful desires, which war against our souls, and would clothe ourselves with the Lord Jesus Christ. Help us to put to death whatever belongs to our earthly natures: sexual immorality, impurity, lust, and evil desires. Amen.

BASED ON JOB 31:1, 1 PETER 2:11, ROMANS 13:14,
AND COLOSSIANS 3:5

10

DATING WITH INTEGRITY

Helping Your Teen Put Together
the Relationship Puzzle

As I write this chapter, I'm sitting in an airport waiting to take a flight back to Nashville, and I can't stop thinking about the teens I met last night at the event where I spoke. This was a smaller venue— only about forty teens were present—but I learned more from this group of teens than I have from any other group in quite some time.

Overall, I'm saddened by what I learned. These teens, who attend church regularly, were all struggling in their dating lives. One teen guy told me he was seriously dating three girls, none of whom had any idea she was being cheated on. One sixteen-year-old girl told me she kisses both guys and girls and thinks it is no big deal. Another girl told me she had just started dating and had already slept with a guy. A sophomore informed me that his girlfriend is pregnant, and he isn't sure if it's his baby or someone else's.

Unfortunately, these situations seem to be representative of today's Christian teenage subculture at large. Remember that trend we talked about—relativism? It's the harmful idea that there is no such thing as absolute right and wrong, and it has spread across the dating world. The line between what's acceptable and what's not has become increasingly blurred.

Turn on the TV or browse through any teen magazine; it won't take long to see that everyone has an opinion to give your teen about dating. Reality TV shows depict dating as a game that can be won by the last contestant standing. Magazine ads insist that teen girls should use their bodies at any cost to attract the attention of guys. Commercials often depict women as products on display to entice the male eye. Teens are bombarded with titillating messages that showcase male and female interaction as lustful and uncontrollable. A generation of teens is being raised with the notion that anything goes when it comes to the opposite sex. Accordingly, a lot of teens today are struggling in their dating lives.

Parent, this is where you step in. Part of your role in fighting for your teen is to help him or her craft a strategy for the dating years. Work with your teen to establish and articulate a reason for dating (Why date in the first place? What does your teen hope to gain by dating?), then set up realistic boundaries that safeguard your teen while out on a date. Think of these safeguards as guidelines for real enjoyment. Truly, dating can be a wonderful time for your teen to develop healthy, God-centered relationships with the opposite sex. Dating can also help your teen develop independence and demonstrate trustworthiness. Your goal is to help your teen develop dating habits that make dating fun and safe while honoring God.

But before moving forward, let's establish this key principle: not every teen has to date, nor is every teen ready to date. It is okay to encourage your teen to hold off from dating. And teens need to know that going solo isn't for losers.

I remember the first time I met Brad. He so impressed me that I included his story in my book *Watch This: A Getting-There Guide to Manhood for Teen Guys*. Brad was the kind of guy that every guy wanted to be and every girl wanted to date. Good looks, good grades, cool car—he had it all. But Brad told me that he wasn't concerned with dating at the moment. He said, "I can't wait to meet the girl I'll spend the rest of my life with. But until then, I'd rather skip all the hassle and temptation of dating. I'm having a blast playing ball, hanging with friends, and just being single."

How refreshing is that!

Sometimes teens believe that they have to date because everyone else does. But teens need to know that it's okay not to date. In fact, choosing not to date frees a teen from all the dating drama and provides a greater sense of focus for developing a strong personality, life skills, and a God-centered worldview.

A Dating Life That Honors God

Your teen might be like Brad—content not to date. But odds are, even if your teen is single now, he or she probably won't be forever. So let's jump in and look at eleven ways you can help your teen establish a solid, God-honoring dating life.

1. Make Sure That When It Comes to Dating, All Conversations Are "On"

Jessica, sixteen, recently e-mailed me this:

> My mom is okay with me dating. I have only been in one serious relationship this year. But there are a lot of questions and

things I'm confused about. She's never really talked to me about guys or any of that stuff. I am thankful she isn't too strict on me. But I also know that I don't have it all figured out myself. What do you think I should do? Should I approach my mom ·and invite her into my personal life? Or should I just keep things the way they are and not risk having her involvement?

Jessica longs for her mom's input. Many teens feel the same way. One mom told me, "I don't push myself on my son. But I do clearly let him know that I am here if and when he wants to talk. And talk is exactly what he has started doing. Early on in his dating years, he didn't tell me a lot. But as he's gotten older, I think he's come to understand that I am safe. We now talk openly about it all, and our relationship is stronger because of it." Isn't this what we all desire as parents—to have a close connection with our teens?

Help your teen know that you'll talk with him or her about any subject. Your teen needs your help, though he or she may never request it, to understand what should and should not happen while on a date. Keep the lines of communication open. Talk to your teen about dating. Ask questions. Encourage your teen to tell you what's happening.

A great place to start talking about dating, especially if your teen is in the early years of dating, is to clearly communicate your expectations. Tell your teen that you will always want to know where your teen is, who your teen is with, and what time he or she will be home.

If your teen is not new to the dating scene, establishing dating guidelines may not sit well at first. Take the time to tell your teen why you want to be more involved in his or her dating life. Explain that you desire more than ever before to help your teen avoid any heartache he or she could experience from making a wrong choice while on a date. Once your teen leaves the house, there is no guarantee that your teen will abide by your wishes. But don't give up. Work to communicate with your teen that you desire to be in the know when it comes to his or her dating experiences.

2. Remind Your Teen That Dating Begins with God

Mom or Dad, always encourage your teen to walk closely with the Lord, particularly when it comes to dating. To have a dating life pleasing to God, your teen must desire a *life* pleasing to God. This happens as your teen commits to consistently communicating with God and seeking His will.

HOW TO LEARN ABOUT YOUR TEEN'S DATING

I have seen many teens make stupid choices while on dates—choices that have often resulted in disaster. So your aim should be to guide your teen through the dating process while also protecting your teen's innocence and future. That takes understanding of what is really going on.

Stay in the loop of your teen's dating experience by:

- inviting your teen's dates over for dinner or to watch a movie
- getting to know the parents of your teen's date
- asking questions about the date—before and after

This is not infringement on your teen's private world. Remember, you are the parent!

As your teen pursues a God-focused life, God will guide and direct your teen throughout his or her dating life. Your teen will be reminded that his or her value and significance is not found in a relationship with someone of the opposite sex; rather, it is found in a committed relationship with Jesus Christ. As your teen develops a deeper relationship with Christ, his or her sense of security will reflect God's plan and purpose for life rather than depend on what a boyfriend or girlfriend wants, expects, or demands from the relationship.

I find that when God is more of a priority in teens' lives, dating becomes less of a priority and more of an option that teens can take or leave. Date or no date, your teen will find identity, purpose, and meaning in God.

3. Offer Practice

Dad, taking your wife out on a date while bringing along your preteen or teen is an excellent teachable moment to help your child better understand what dating should be about. Seeing you opening the door, pulling out a chair, being respectful, complimenting, and making sure to avoid taking your date to any unsafe environment can be ways for your son to view how he should treat girls on his dates. This can be a powerful teachable moment for your daughter as well as she sees first-hand how she should expect and demand to be treated by a guy on her future dates. One father recently told me about his experiences:

> As a learning experience, I recently took my wife on a date and double-dated with my fourteen-year-old son, Josh, and my eleven-year-old daughter. The first part of the date was a total disaster. Josh had no intentions of treating Sarah, his sister, with respect. Realizing my plan was not working, I switched dates with Josh

and had him continue the date night with his mom as his date. The rest of the evening was a powerful learning experience for Josh and us all. He treated his mom with the utmost respect—pulling out her chair at the restaurant for her, opening the door for her to get into the car, and more. And get this: Josh even asked us if he could take his mom on another date again soon.

What an excellent way for your teen to experience what it means to respect, and be respected by, a date!

4. Encourage Group Dates

If you're not yet comfortable with allowing your teen to date, you may want to consider letting him or her group date. Group dating allows your teen to begin dating in the presence of others and with certain restrictions. As your teen proves more trustworthy, then you can give more dating freedom.

You get to set the restrictions for group dating. Allowing your teen to date while at a youth event where a youth pastor and other parents are present or dropping your teen off at the mall or youth event to meet a date or group of friends are possibilities. The options are limitless.

Another form of encouraging group dating, especially for a teen who has never dated, is to require that your teen date at home first. One father told me that whenever his daughter begins a new dating relationship, he requires her to spend the first three dates at home. This allows him and his wife the opportunity to meet their daughter's new crush. He stated, "Most guys make it through the first and sometimes the second date, but few make it through all three."

True colors always show themselves. If his daughter does not mean enough to the new guy for the guy to be willing to abide by this father's dating rules and stick around for the third date, then he most likely is not the right one to date his daughter.

5. Encourage Conversation-Focused Dating

Encourage your teen to focus on spending time in conversation with his or her date. For instance, spending quality time at a restaurant or at the mall talking will help your teen begin to know his or her date better. This will also help your teen better understand the character qualities he or she desires from someone in a dating relationship.

The key is to make sure your teen dates in atmospheres conducive to producing good conversation. The following statement may sound strong, but it's true: going to a movie can be one of the worst possible dates. Think about it. When your teen goes to a movie with a date, it puts your teen in an environment where he or she spends two hours seated close to a member of the opposite sex in a dark room, often holding hands, without saying anything. Even the most innocent of movies can place your teen in an environment that may lead to a physical encounter, either right then in the theater or at a later point on the date.

It's key to encourage your teen to choose activities that keep him or her away from environments that encourage physical encounters. Even when your teen is not desiring to end the date by getting physical, it can be challenging if your teen is in an environment that encourages physical intimacy. Parked cars, couches in darkened basements, bedrooms with closed doors—these are dangerous environments that will cause the strongest of teens to struggle.

The goal of any date for your teen should be to focus the relationship on honoring God. Help your teen avoid environments of temptation and focus the date on conversation and fun.

6. Know Your Teen's Dating Patterns

As your teen starts dating, he or she will develop an individual perspective on dating. Where is *your* teen at with dating? Ask yourself:

- *Does my teen care little about dating, or is my teen desperate for a date?*
- *When my teen gets involved in a relationship, does he or she strive to make sure the relationship works at all costs?*
- *Does my teen bounce from one relationship to the next, always looking for the quick thrill of dating a new person?*
- *Is my teen interested in waiting to date until he or she has met "the one"?*
- *Does my teen view dating just as a fun time of hanging out with friends?*
- *Does my teen quickly fall in and out of love (that is, what he or she believes is love)?*

The answers to such questions are important in helping you better understand how your teen views dating. Being aware of your teen's dating habits can help you recognize when your teen might be developing unhealthy patterns that could lead to danger. For instance, if your daughter is insecure about herself and believes that a boyfriend will make her more secure, then she may be willing to do whatever she believes is necessary to hold on to a boyfriend. Or if your son views dating as a game of hooking up, then he may be developing a harmful pattern of using girls.

The better connected you stay with your teen, the better prepared you will be to help your teen maneuver through the dating process.

7. Pray Before Each Date

Praying with your teen is a critical step to helping your teen establish and maintain dating relationships that honor God. In Luke 22:40, Jesus challenged His disciples by saying, "Pray that you will not fall into temptation." That's the kind of prayer we're talking about.

This step isn't for wimps. I'll admit that when I tell a roomful of teens to pray with their parents before dates, there usually are a few teens who give me a hard time.

My encouragement is for you to take the lead on this with your teen. Prayer changes everything. It sets the tone for the date and helps your teen establish a God-centered foundation for the relationship.

8. Urge Your Teen to Date Only Other Christians

One of the most consistent questions Christian teens ask me about their dating lives is if it is okay to date someone who is not a Christian. I typically answer this question with other questions: "Would you want to marry someone who doesn't follow Christ? Would you want to marry someone who wouldn't embrace reading the Bible, going to church, and praying? Would you want to marry someone who wouldn't teach your children godly character and to pray, go to church, and read the Bible?"

Then I follow up with some advice like this: "I hope the answer to each of these questions is a definite no. If this is the case, then why would you choose to date someone who wouldn't do these things? I'm not saying you have to think you're going to marry every person you go out with. But every person you date should be marriage worthy. And the first question on the marriage-worthy test should always be, is this person a Christian?"

Parent, I believe this is one of those no-compromise areas. Second Corinthians 6:14–16 says, "Don't become partners with those who reject God. How can you make a partnership out of right and wrong? That's not partnership; that's war. Is light best friends with dark? Does Christ go strolling with the Devil? Do trust and mistrust hold hands? Who would think of setting up pagan idols in God's holy Temple? But that is exactly what we are, each of us a temple in whom God lives" (MSG).

Dating a non-Christian might seem innocent. Sometimes a teen believes that after a while he or she will "win the person over" to Christ, but that's a dangerous idea to trust in, because hearts get entangled while dating. The Bible warns that people walk on dangerous ground when they choose to unite (even just for a few dates) with those who reject God.

One student recently said to me, "Jeffrey, that is being judgmental and intolerant. We are taught in our church to love everyone and accept everyone. Who are you to judge others and say that I can't spend time with them?"

My response: "I most definitely am not saying you should never spend time with this person. It's not an issue of judging another or not accepting another. It is an issue of *partnering with him or her* in a relationship that could develop into a lifelong commitment. This doesn't mean that you are turning your back on an individual or not accepting this person or choosing not to love him or her. What it does mean is that you are striving to protect God's temple, your body, from becoming something God never intended it to be."

Jesus spent time with the lowest of the low while He walked this planet. He dined with prostitutes, liars, thieves, murderers, and the like. But He did so not to partner with them but rather to point them to His Father. There is a huge distinction between *accepting* one who is lost and *partnering* with one who is lost.

9. Help Set Boundaries for Physical Acts

Teens often ask me "How far is too far?" It's an age-old question, one that sometimes has been inadvertently muddied by well-meaning speakers hoping to put new twists on the idea by talking to youth about purity, heart, and intention. These are good issues to discuss (we'll do so in chapter 11), but the physical-boundary question also deserves a simple, straightforward, and memorable answer for your teen.

The clearest way to answer this question is to say, "Never touch any part of a body covered by a bathing suit." Or "Draw imaginary lines at a person's shoulders and knees—never touch anything between those two lines." I think it's also important to spell out that activities such as handholding or sharing a brief hug or a brief kiss on the cheek or lips may be appropriate in a dating relationship. But activities such as prolonged hugging and kissing, French kissing, touching breasts, petting and fondling of clothed or unclothed genital areas, mutual masturbation, oral sex, any sort of nudity, anal intercourse, and genital intercourse are not acceptable before marriage.

Parent, it's perfectly okay to spell these things out for your teen clearly, simply, and directly. The world is already talking about these things with your teen. Your teen needs to hear about appropriate boundaries from you.

Setting boundaries is where many teens fail. You and your teen can apply every other step in this chapter to his or her dating life, but if you do not help your teen set boundaries, it will only be a matter of time before he or she gets tripped up.

10. Help Develop an Exit Plan

I tell teens often, "You cannot wait for a fire to get started to figure out how you are going to escape. What I mean is, you cannot wait until you're already in a tempting or compromising situation to figure out how to avoid it."

Before your teen's next date, he or she needs to do the following:

- Be clear on what type of events he or she will and will not attend. For example, your teen may say, "We will never be alone in a tempting environment, such as a bedroom."
- Be ready and able to say no.
- Be willing and ready to exit from a relationship if your teen finds himself or herself in a relationship that does not honor God.

One grandfather told me that he always gave his daughter a dime before she left on her dates. If she found herself in an environment in which she needed to quickly leave, she could call him at anytime from anywhere. This same principle works today, but with a cell phone. Clearly communicate to your teen that he or she can call you at any time, day or night, from anywhere, and you will come and pick the teen up.

11. Teach Your Teen Never to Compromise

I meet parents everywhere who are scared that their teens will make the same foolish choices they made when they were younger. A mom in tears I met backstage at an event told me, "I made some awful choices when I was a teen that haunt me still to this day. I am so afraid that my daughter is going to buy the same lies I did and find herself years from now living with the same regrets I have."

I am confident that every parent desires to help his or her teen avoid making regrettable choices during the dating years. How can you do this with your teen? Don't stop communicating these two words: *never compromise!*

I often challenge teens to consider the kind of person they desire to marry one day. This simple exercise helps them develop a vision for what's ahead and provides a gauge by which they can determine whether or not someone is dateable. Then they can apply the no-compromise principle.

But what if your teen has already compromised?

Beginning Again

I've met many teens who believe that because of past mistakes on dates, they can never start over. This is a powerful trap from Satan. He has lured many teens into believing they cannot honor God in their future dating lives. But the truth is, God's forgiveness is not conditional. When we ask for it, He is ready and willing to give it. "If we confess our sins, he is faithful and just and will forgive us our sins and purify us from all unrighteousness" (1 John 1:9). God says, "I will forgive you," period.

If your teen has made mistakes in the past, he or she needs to know that every day is a new day with God. Your teen needs his or her own Sweeping Aside Motion. The past is the past. The important thing is to avoid making the same wrong choices again.

In the New Testament, we read how Jesus commanded a woman caught in adultery, "Go now and leave your life of sin" (John 8:11). Good advice for all of us who have sinned.

Your teen may need to take extreme measures to avoid being in the same environment where he or she previously failed. This may mean walking away from a harmful dating relationship. Unless your teen takes drastic measures to avoid repeating certain mistakes, he or she may find himself or herself in a vicious cycle of constantly failing in the same areas.

Give your teen encouragement when he or she is feeling guilty. It can make all the difference in where the teen's dating life goes in the future.

Sticking in There

Parent, one of the foundational principles of this book is that your teen wants you to be involved. Remember, your teen may not always show it, but your being interested in what interests your teen is important to your teen.

As you strive to communicate better with your teen about his or her dating life, you may encounter a negative response at first. But do not throw in the towel. Using your Deep Breath Posture, keep patiently pushing into the life of your teen. Be creative. Take it slow at first if necessary. Let your teen build trust in your interest in his or her dating life.

You're winning the fight.

Praying Scripture for Your Teen

Father, I pray that You would create in my teen a pure heart and renew a steadfast spirit within my teen. I pray that whatever is true, whatever is noble, whatever is right, whatever is pure, whatever is lovely, whatever is admirable—if anything is excellent or praiseworthy—my teen would think about such things. I pray that my teen would flee from sexual immorality. Help my teen in this area. Help me be the parent I need to be. Amen.

BASED ON PSALM 51:10, PHILIPPIANS 4:8,
AND 1 CORINTHIANS 6:18

11

TALKING ABOUT SEX

The Crucial Conversation
Your Teen Needs...from You

This isn't the kind of talk most people expect when they open the pages of the Bible, but it's there:

> Oh yes! Your breasts
> > will be clusters of sweet fruit to me,
> Your breath clean and cool like fresh mint,
> > your tongue and lips like the best wine.
> > > (Song of Solomon 7:8–9, MSG)

Racy stuff in that biblical book about marriage!

In the Bible we see that sexuality was God's idea in the first place. So why do parents often find it hard to talk to their teens about sex? Have you ever heard yourself say something like the following statements?

- "No one talked to me when I was young, and I did just fine."
- "My teen doesn't even think about sex!"

- "If I talk to my teen about sex, he'll want to try it."
- "I'm leaving it up to my wife."
- "I'm leaving it up to my husband."
- "This is the church's responsibility."
- "My teen is too young."
- "I don't know what to say."

It sounds surprising, but the teens I talk to say that down deep they actually want their parents to have this talk with them, even though it is sometimes an awkward conversation to have.

My parents talked to my older brother and me about sex when I was about nine. I can still remember the scene at the kitchen table. My brother and I tried to look anywhere except in our parents' eyes. There was a lot of squirming—on our parents' side as well as ours. So I recognize the possibility for discomfort.

But still, this is a conversation that needs to happen. If you as a Christian parent don't talk to your son or daughter, who will? Satan and his demons are already waging a war in this area. Your teen's body and mind are changing, and evil spirits are using the world around your teen to bombard him or her with images that are contrary to God's plan.

So, how do you go about having this crucial conversation with your teen? What do you say? How do you become the number one source of ongoing wisdom for your teen in the area of sexuality? It starts with keeping the lines of communication open so that this conversation happens more than once.

From "the Talk" to "the Talks"

A question parents often ask me is, "How can I keep my teen from having sex?" The sad but true answer is, "You can't!" Parents can do all the right things, and teens still may become sexually active before marriage. But although you cannot control your teen's choices, you can control your involvement in helping your teen make the right choices.

I have heard some parents make the comment, "My teen has had enough of the sex talk for a while." In this case the teen usually has just been to an abstinence rally, or perhaps he or she has gone through a book or listened to a speaker on this topic at a youth-group gathering recently.

But I'd say that a good rule of thumb regarding the frequency of talking to your teen about sex is about once a month. Yep, you heard me right—once a month.

Sadly, parents are often stuck in the mind-set of having "the talk," singular.

At a parent event where I spoke recently, a father told me, "I had the talk with my son when he was eleven. It was difficult to get through it. But I did it."

I congratulated the dad, then asked him, "How old is your son now?"

"Seventeen," he replied.

You have to talk with your teen about sex way more often than that. Why? Because your teen is constantly being bombarded with messages about sexuality from sources other than you. You will lose this fight if you believe a one-time conversation is all it takes.

This is an area where it is true that we are living in a different world than the world you and I knew as teens. It is an understatement to say that teens are slammed with sexual messages today. Our fight must be equally aggressive and unapologetic in communicating truths to our teens. It's no longer about "the talk." It is about consistent communication.

What Your Teen Needs to Know

Overwhelmingly, teens tell me that their parents are the single most influential factor in their sexual decision making. This tells me that teens not only want to talk to Mom and Dad about this stuff but also value what Mom and Dad have to say.

So where do you start? I'll leave the specifics of what you say up to you. But let me offer nine broader themes that need to be communicated to your teen.

1. Your Teen Needs to Know That You Are Approachable and Unshockable

Can your teen ask you anything? *Anything?* If not, then you must create an environment of approachability that clearly communicates to your teen that he or she can come to you and get answers to any questions or concerns related to sexuality.

Recently I spoke with a seventeen-year-old girl who lives with her divorced father. At age thirteen she started becoming physical with a boy three years older. On several occasions she approached her father, who would not discuss the topic with her. Instead, he simply put her on birth control. She hopped around from one guy to the next. Though she never became pregnant, she did develop a sexually transmitted disease that eventually led to her cervix being removed.

The point: your teen needs to see you as safe. Your teen needs to know that if he or she comes to you with any question or any concern, you will talk with him or her about what's truly going on.

If this is a new idea to you, take some time alone with your teen and work to communicate exactly this point. Let your teen know that you are new to this area and that things may be somewhat uncomfortable at first for both of you. But let your teen know that you are willing and desiring to be the one he or she comes to. You welcome your teen's questions, no matter how weird, scary, embarrassing, or shocking they may seem.

2. Your Teen Needs to Know What You Expect Regarding Sexual Behavior

Alycia, seventeen, recently e-mailed me: "I really believe I will be a virgin on the day of my wedding. My parents have always talked with me about waiting. They challenged me to wait for that one special person. I'm not saying it's always easy, but I am committed, thanks to the input I received from my parents." That's a great e-mail.

At a recent parenting conference, I asked parents to raise their hands if they desired their teens to be virgins on their wedding nights. The auditorium was immediately filled with hands in the air. Then I asked, "How many of you have told your teens within the last month that you want them to be virgins on their wedding nights?" Less than 3 percent of hands remained in the air.

My encouragement here is to clearly and consistently articulate your expectations in this area to your child. It does not matter if your child is ten, sixteen, or twenty-two. If he or she is not married, your son or daughter needs to hear from you consistently that you expect him or her to wait until marriage to have sex.

3. Your Teen Needs to Know What You Believe

Consider this question: do you believe that there is ever a time when it is okay to have sex outside of marriage, such as if a couple are in love, have dated for a long time, or are engaged? This is a critical question that you must solidify an answer to in your mind and heart before talking with your teen.

A verse that I often show teens when discussing what the Bible says about their sexuality is 1 Corinthians 6:18: "Flee from sexual immorality." The Greek word for sexual immorality here is *porneia,* which refers to all sexual sin. God is saying, "Run from all sexual sin." God does not say run from it unless you are in love or engaged or really care about each other. He says run from it, period!

As a parent, you must be convinced that sexual sin is sin, no matter the situation, no matter how in love the couple feel. Take your teen to this verse, and show him or her *the truth*—God's Word. Then lead your teen to live by it.

4. Your Teen Needs to Know the Positive Side of the Story

Teens consistently tell me that they are sick of hearing everyone say, "Don't have sex!" Why? Because most of the pro-abstinence information they receive today is negative.

The teens have a good point!

I find that many well-intentioned adults, abstinence educators, pastors, and parents mainly focus on the negative side when trying to convince their teens to say no to sex. And most people, especially teens, do not respond well to negative persuasion. Focusing on the positive aspects of waiting and the reward that follows will make a much stronger case than only driving home the consequences that come from sex outside marriage.

Look at what Heather, fifteen, told me: "I know sex outside of marriage is wrong. I've heard that from Mom, Dad, church, teachers, my pastor, and more for years! Everyone has told me the bad. But I wish someone would spin it positive. I don't think I've ever heard my parents or pastor once tell me something really good about sex. If sex is such a great thing from God, then why don't we hear about how great it is?"

Work to share with your teen the positive aspects of waiting until marriage. If you waited, share with your teen the joy that brought into your wedding night. No guilt, no comparison to a previous relationship, and no concern over emotional baggage or disease!

Sex is an amazing gift from God. When teens choose to protect this gift and keep it within the context of His plan, there are rewards that follow. As you begin to communicate this message with your teen, you *then* can show how following God's plan will eliminate the possibility of hurt, pain, emotional scars, diseases, and unwanted pregnancies.

God's plan is not designed to keep us from having fun. It is meant to protect us.

5. Your Teen Needs to Know About You

I have often been asked by parents, "How much should I tell my teen about my past?"

This issue has been debated by authors, counselors, doctors, pastors, and more, and I realize this is a sensitive question. I have read and researched legitimate answers that support both sides well. And the fact is, whether or not you disclose to your teen such sensitive information about your past is a call that ultimately you have to make.

But here are several things to consider that may help you in making the right call for you and your teen.

You are real. Here's a fact: I am not the greatest communicator in the world. There are speakers who speak better than I do, have a greater understanding of the Bible, and are funnier, smarter, and more entertaining.

But I know that teens listen to me. Why? Because I show them I'm real. I'm quick to admit that I'm still learning. I'm not satisfied with where I am. I want to be a better man. I want to give God more of me today than I gave Him previously. I'm not perfect, and I'm still capable of making really poor choices—but I own up to my mistakes. Teens see me as someone who, just like them, doesn't have it all together.

Does your teen see you as someone who is real? You don't have to be perfect to be real. Some of the teens I talk to believe their parents never did anything wrong, so the teens mistakenly believe their parents never faced the struggles they are facing. The teens conclude their parents would not understand or would be disappointed in knowing their struggles and failures.

You understand. Even though teens' temptations are packaged differently today than ours were, teens still face many of the same struggles you and I faced at their age. What a powerful tool you have—your past—in helping your teen see that you understand where he or she is now because you were there! I am not saying that you need to expose all of the skeletons in the closet of your past, but I am saying that there can be power in discussing your teen years: what temptations you faced, what you thought about sex, or possibly even how desperate you felt for someone to talk to during that time.

Teens want to know that you understand what is going on in their lives. Helping them realize that you have been where they now walk may help them see you as someone who is approachable.

You are forgiven. If you have never discussed the topic of sex with your teen because of the wrong choices you have made in your life, remember, the past is over (Sweeping Aside Motion). If you have gone to God with your past, seeking forgiveness and freedom, then believe what He says in 1 John 1:8–9: "If we claim that we're free of sin, we're only fooling ourselves. A claim like that is errant nonsense. On the other hand, if we admit our sins—make a clean breast of them—he won't let us down; he'll be true to himself. He'll forgive our sins and purge us of all wrongdoing" (MSG).

Some people say that if you choose to share your past sexual mistakes with your teen, he or she may respond, "Well, you did not wait until marriage to have sex, and you turned out okay." And this may be the response of your teen. But if so, you will then have an opportunity to share the hurt you have experienced from these choices. God's forgiveness frees you to do this.

You are responsible only to God. Some parents feel as though they should share everything about the past with their teen. Others feel as though they should never do so. But it doesn't matter what others have done—it only matters what God wants you to do. This is between you and God long before it is between you and your teen.

If you are considering talking with your teen about your past, then before you do anything else, do this:

- Ask God if, and how, He would have you use your past as a tool to communicate His plan for your teen's sex life.
- Make sure you aren't using your teen's ear for the benefit of your own emotional recovery. Your intentions should be fully to help your teen in his or her journey and not to unload your own guilt and pain from the past.
- Realize that questions may follow your talk with your teen, and so be prepared for them. If your teen asks a question you cannot fully answer or you aren't sure how to answer at this point, be honest. Take some time to work through the answer, then return to your teen to continue the conversation.

God may want to use your past to help in protecting the future of your teen. You need to be sensitive to God's leading in this matter. And if you are sensing this is His will, then no matter how difficult it may seem, know that at the right time God will provide the right words for you to speak and the ears for your teen to listen.

6. Your Teen Needs to Know It's Not Just About Virginity

It may sound strange, but Amy and I are *not* praying that our children will be virgins on their wedding days. Instead, we are praying for their purity. Why? The word *virgin* can inadvertently become an escape word for teens, one that gives them a false sense of appropriateness in their behavior. There are many physical acts that a teen can do on dates without going "all the way" or losing his or her "virginity" that can be just as damaging spiritually, physically, and emotionally.

The number one question about sex teens ask me is, "How far is too far?" (For a more complete answer on this question, see chapter 10.) What the teen is often asking here is, "How far can I go without getting into trouble?" or "How much can I get away with?" Your teen needs to clearly understand that this question can be dangerous because this "How close to the danger can I dance before I fall" approach will eventually take him or her down a path to tragedy. Our bodies were never created for us to be able to do whatever we want on our dates, physically, and then just draw the line and stop. This is why God warns us in 1 Corinthians to avoid *porneia*—any sexual sin—at all cost. We can't even have a hint of it, as Ephesians 5:3 says, because God understands that sometimes all it takes is just a little to push you over the edge.

Remember, the key here is purity. Challenging your teen to pursue a lifestyle of purity will help your teen understand that better than asking, "How close can I get?" he or she needs to be asking, "How far away do I need to stay?"

For some teens, a kiss can get them into trouble. For others, all it takes is too long a hug or a touch on the leg. Even if your teen doesn't share with you such an intimate revelation about the "ledge" from which he or she can fall, you can help your teen understand how impor-

tant it is to know where that ledge is so the teen can make a commitment to never approach it.

7. Your Teen Needs to Know That the World's Good Never Trumps God's Best

God wants your teen to experience His very best. This is true in every
aspect of life, including the area of sex. But many teens I talk to believe
that if they can come up with "good" reasons to have sex, then it must
be okay. I have heard countless excuses from teens as to why they have
sex before marriage, including these:

- "I'm in love."
- "We planned ahead."
- "I'm old enough now."
- "Everyone else does."
- "It was prom night."
- "We are practicing safe sex." (This is the most common excuse
  I hear.)

Teens need to know that no matter how good it seems in the
moment, nothing is ever okay that is out of God's will for their lives.
No matter how cool sex looks on TV, no matter how romantic a sex
scene is in the latest movie, no matter how glamorous or exciting MTV
makes sex look, the world's good never trumps God's best.

After I had spoken about sex at a high school recently, a girl
approached me and said, "Jeffrey, I agree with everything you had to say
today. But you don't understand. My boyfriend and I have a really good
thing going." She then proceeded to explain to me for several minutes
that they were in love, had dated for several years, were going to get
married soon, and so on. In her mind, all of these reasons justified her
desire to have sex with him now.

Parent, God is not in the business of just making sure that your teen has a good relationship with the person he or she is dating. God wants your teen to have the *best* future! In order to have the best in the future, there are times when your teen must be willing to say no to what seems good right now.

8. Your Teen Needs to Know How to Say No

"How do I say no without hurting his feelings?" This is a popular question that I hear from teen girls. Many teen girls desire to say no to their boyfriends' physical advances, but many are afraid of hurting the boys' feelings.

I have one word for these girls: tough. Hurt his feelings!

I often tell teens, "You cannot wait until you are in the moment and things begin to really heat up on your date to decide whether you are going to say no and how you are going to say it. You must be ready. Learn how to say no. *No* is a good word!"

Before your teen ever leaves the house for that party on Friday night, or before that date ever begins, your teen must have a plan. This is true whether we are talking about sex, alcohol, drugs, or watching a certain movie or video.

As you have probably seen time and again, teens typically do not have a problem speaking their minds. We need to teach them to use this boldness in an effective way to say no to sex and anything else that is against God's will for their lives.

9. Your Teen Needs to Know That Tomorrow Is a New Day

One of the biggest lies Satan wants to sell your teen is the lie that your teen's past is an indicator of his or her future. But as we saw in a previous chapter, no matter where your teen has been or what your teen has done, the past is over. If your teen has made poor choices sexually, your teen can begin again. Some call that secondary virginity. One teen told me he called it being "revirginized"! I call it forgiveness through grace.

Point your teen to God for forgiveness and healing. Then help your teen establish a game plan for the future so he or she can avoid making the same mistakes again. Help your teen establish boundaries and determine to embrace God's plan.

Power, Love, and Self-Control

All of this talk about sexuality may seem awkward at first, or perhaps even elementary, to both you and your teen. And even having repeated discussions will not guarantee that your son or daughter will follow the game plan. But it will begin to establish in the mind of your teen that you mean business and are ready to fight to help your teen win the sexual war that the forces of evil are waging against him or her.

Let me encourage you to take up your Ultimate Power Stance and pray 2 Timothy 1:7, specifically, for your teen: "God did not give us a spirit of timidity, but a spirit of power, of love and of self-discipline." Pray that your teen will not be timid in this area. Pray that God would develop in your teen a passion for courage, honor, and integrity. Pray that your teen will have a love for God that burns stronger than any other love in his or her heart. Pray that this love would develop in him or her a spirit of self-control. Pray that, when tempted, your teen would rely on God's power to stand for righteousness.

Now you're really fighting.

Praying Scripture for Your Teen

Dear Lord, I pray that You would give my teen a spirit of power, love, and self-discipline. I pray that my teen would flee from sexual immorality. Help me as a parent know how to talk—and continue talking—about this subject with my teen. Amen.

BASED ON 2 TIMOTHY 1:7 AND 1 CORINTHIANS 6:18

12

THE DRINKING GAME

It's Been Around Forever, but It's Got a New Set of Rules

I recently overheard a cell-phone conversation (the phone was set on speakerphone, almost as if this student wanted others to hear) while in a crowd of students at a public high school. The conversation went like this:

TEEN GUY TALKING INTO PHONE: "So, are you going tonight?"

TEEN GIRL ON SPEAKERPHONE: "Of course. Everyone's going. I can't wait. Where are you going to tell your parents you'll be tonight? You know you'll be too far gone to drive home."

GUY: "I'll just tell them that I'm spending the night at Tyler's. What about you? What will you tell your mom?"

GIRL: "Oh, my mom's cool. She hardly ever asks where I am. As long as I call her at some point tonight, she's okay with whatever."

GUY: "Cool. See you there. It's gonna rock!"

Conversations like that are nothing new. Whenever a big party is being planned, it seems like it's the only thing being talked about by teens for days leading up to it. What starts out as a few friends getting together for a good time often turns into a lot more than just movies, popcorn, and Cokes.

Unfortunately, I hear these types of things when I hang around with Christian kids as well. Sometimes the conversations will be more muffled, but it's hard to quell the buzz: Who's coming? Who's going to bring the beer? How many shots will it take before someone passes out? What will you tell your parents about where you will be? Who will you hook up with? What will you remember tomorrow? Where will you crash until you sober up?

Drugs and alcohol are nothing new. Teens will be teens, right?

One father said to me, "I drank some and smoked a little weed when I was in high school, and I turned out okay. What's the big deal with partying with your high-school buddies every now and then?"

I know that you want the best for your teen. I also know that many teens (and some parents) have bought the lie that a casual drink or puff is innocent. But the danger behind drugs and alcohol is real and deep. Satan is winning the war in the lives of many teens by encouraging them to dabble in the dark world of drugs and alcohol.

Recently I conducted a small, nonscientific experiment. I watched a professional basketball game on TV and counted all the commercials for beer. In three hours I counted fifteen beer commercials. That's five an hour. Basically I was shown one beer commercial during every single commercial break.

That's just one example of the plethora of messages being thrown at us today, insisting that consuming alcohol is as innocent as drinking soda. Satan is so clever at making harmful stuff look good.

But what's the truth? The Bible says, "Wine is a mocker and beer a brawler" (Proverbs 20:1), and, "Do not join those who drink too much wine" (Proverbs 23:20). The Bible is also clear in 1 Corinthians 6:10 that neither "thieves nor the greedy *nor drunkards* nor slanderers nor swindlers will inherit the kingdom of God" (emphasis added).

Why are drugs and alcohol dangerous? When teens use such substances and become drunk or stoned, they can get hurt. Sometimes they become addicted. Sometimes they die or cause accidents that kill others. There are legal issues involved—your teen can be arrested, undergo a strip search, spend time in juvenile lockup, be forced to pay fines, and have a record that harms the teen's ability to vote, be accepted into some colleges, and get certain jobs. And then there are spiritual dangers. Drugs and alcohol cause people to lose control of themselves. They become distanced from God and from what matters most. Just once I'd like to see all that in a TV commercial for beer!

Several years ago I met a high-school sophomore named Chad at a Christian high school in California. I assumed he was a football player just by looking at him. As he began to tell me his story, he fought to hold back the tears. By the time the story was over, I fought to do the same.

When Chad was a freshman, his brother was a senior. After the first game of the season, Chad went to a party with his brother. "I still remember seeing my brother drink that night," Chad said. "I had never seen him drink before. When he handed me a beer, I just took it. Everyone there was doing it. And I didn't want to be the only one not doing it."

One beer led to many more. "Every Friday night was another game, another party," Chad said. "By the time the football season was over, I had downed a lot more than just beer. Tequila, Jack and Coke, shots—we did it all."

During Christmas break of his freshman year, Chad and his brother both had a few beers at a friend's house. His brother passed out. So Chad, without a license yet and drunk himself, decided to drive home.

With his brother in the passenger seat, Chad blew through a stop sign and crashed into another vehicle. His brother was ejected from the car and killed on impact.

"The worst part of it all is knowing each day that I made a stupid decision that ended my brother's life," Chad said.

It's easy to dismiss a story like Chad's as being a tragic exception to the rule. But over the years I've heard *a lot* of stories involving teens and drugs and alcohol that I'd categorize as tragic. Accidents happen more often than you think. Hell's horde want nothing more than to see your teen end up exactly like Chad's brother. That's why they are raising the stakes. And if you haven't heard, they have been pretty successful with this generation in getting alcohol and drugs into the hands of teens.

So, what's a parent to do? How can you be successful in fighting this battle alongside your teen?

Trends in Teen Experimentation

Hang around teens long enough, and you will hear all the reasons why teens experiment with drugs and alcohol. In a recent conversation with a group of Christian teens, I asked them why they drank or used drugs. Here's what they said:

- "Why do I use pot? Everybody does in my school."
- "If I don't drink, I won't get invited to other parties."
- "It's been a hell of a year for me. I drink because I deserve it."
- "It's really easy to get drugs at my school. We all know who has it. And we all know what parties to attend to find it."
- "Finals are over, and I want to unwind with my friends."
- "I was a virgin and was thinking about sleeping with my boyfriend, and I thought one drink would relax me."

In fifteen years of working with teens, I have unfortunately met few teens—Christian or otherwise—whom I have questioned about drinking, smoking pot, or trying other drugs who told me they have never experimented. Teens often fail to see the link between choices and consequences. They have a tendency to feel indestructible and immune to anything beyond the moment.

Put your Open Book Motion into play, and learn about the teen culture of drug abuse. Here are two trends I'm seeing in this area.

1. Teens Are Misusing Legal Drugs

Some of the drugs teens abuse can be found right in your own home. These include inhalants; fumes from glues, aerosols, and solvents; over-the-counter cough, cold, sleep, and diet medications; and prescribed medications.

One Christian mom recently said to me, "I never thought my kid would do drugs, especially in my own home."

"Where did he get them?" I asked.

"Right from my bathroom," she said. "He took my pain prescription from a surgery I had and started taking them like candy."

What this mom is referring to is a growing trend among teens today known as *pharming*. Teens take legal prescription drugs they find at home.

When I was a teen, I knew who did drugs in my school. Back then, teens usually had to find a dealer, develop trust in that person, then pay the street price for their drug of choice. Today, trafficking is simply about whatever prescription drugs you can find in the bathroom cabinet. Teens sell or trade drugs to friends and classmates. Unfortunately, the madness doesn't stop there.

Another trend is called *party pharming*. This usually happens at invitation-only, weekend parties. Teens raid their home medicine cabinets and come prepared to share the harvest with other attendees. Once at the party, the teens put whatever prescription pills they have in a bowl and help themselves. Considering that users cannot identify different medications or dosage amounts, recklessly reaching into a bowl of pills can be deadly. But, of course, that is the thrill of a *pharm party*—you never know what ride you'll get taken on.

2. Date-Rape Drugs Are Prevalent

Here's what one sixteen-year-old girl recently e-mailed me:

> I went to a party with my best friend when I was a sophomore.
> We didn't know the guy who was throwing the party, but we
> had heard everyone would be there. I met a lot of cute guys and
> eventually got separated from Ashley [her friend she attended
> the party with]. I don't remember everything that happened that
> night. At some point early the next morning, I woke up outside,
> lying on a blanket in the backyard. My pants were off, and I
> knew someone had had sex with me. I don't know who it was,
> but I know I didn't want to lose my virginity. I'm pretty sure
> someone slipped something in my drink and then raped me.

Statistics show that most date rapes happen while the victim is under the influence of alcohol. Yet there are also two drugs commonly known as date-rape drugs: GHB and benzodiazepines (such as flunitrazepam or Rohypnol, also known by teens as roofies, rophy, ruffles, ruffies, ruff up, forget it, and the forget-me pill). Here are the facts about these drugs:

Is Your Teen a User?

How do you know if your teen is into alcohol or drugs? Here are some common signs to watch for:

- the odor of alcohol on clothes, on breath, or in a car
- a sudden change in mood or attitude
- poor performance in school, in sports, or at work
- depression
- fatigue
- repeated health complaints
- red and glazed eyes
- loss of interest in school, sports, or other activities
- discipline problems
- lack of interest in family and friends
- secrecy
- association with a new group of friends and a reluctance to introduce them to you
- alcohol or prescription drugs disappearing from your home
- low self-esteem or irresponsible behavior
- starting arguments, breaking rules, or having problems with the law
- change in appearance, dress, or hair

- These two drugs are virtually undetectable when slipped into a drink. They are tasteless, odorless, and colorless.

- All traces of the drugs will leave the body within seventy-two hours of ingestion.

- They are not detected in any routine toxicology screen or blood test.

- The victim is unconscious but responsive, with little or no memory of what happens.

- These drugs can make the victim act without inhibition, often in an affectionate or sexual way.

- These drugs render a person incapable of thinking clearly or making appropriate decisions.

- These drugs can also cause such effects as dizziness, nausea, unconsciousness, seizures, breathing problems, tremors, slow heart rate, coma, and even death.

The use of date-rape drugs along with pharming are just a couple of the reasons why we need to wake up to what's going on with teens today—and why we need to do something about drug and alcohol use related to our own teens.

Safety: A False Assumption

A seventeen-year-old named Reilly told me that he had been smoking pot since he was in eighth grade. I asked him if his parents knew.

"No way," he said. "They have no idea. I've even done it at home."

"How have you kept this a secret from your parents for so long?" I asked.

"They never asked," he said.

Reilly was involved in church, was popular, and was a star athlete at school. Reilly's parents assumed that because he was excelling in so many areas of his life, drugs surely would never be a factor.

Maybe you know that your teen is already drinking or taking drugs. Or maybe you know for sure that your teen is not doing those things. But if there's even a chance that you have a Reilly on your hands, don't wait. Talk to your teen now. In particular, consider establishing a written or verbal contract including such commitments as the following:

- I will not drink or try drugs.
- I will not ride in a car with anyone who has been drinking or is under the influence.
- I will not allow anyone to ride in my car who has been drinking or is under the influence.

The contract also can spell out other agreements. For example, if you find out that someone drank or used drugs in your car while your teen was behind the wheel, you could establish a penalty like suspending driving privileges for two months. By discussing the prohibitions and the penalties with your teen and by documenting the discussion in a contract, you eliminate surprises and make your expectations clear. And it's important that if your teen messes up, you make sure to follow through on discipline.

Fighting for Your Teen

There's a lot of information out there about the dangers of drug and alcohol abuse. Your teen doesn't need a dissertation on the subject. What your teen needs is your consistent voice.

I believe many teens want to do right. They just need constant reassurance from Mom and Dad. So look for moments of opportunity to instill in your teen the truths discussed in this chapter. Don't buy the Enemy's lie that one talk will cut it with your teen. Don't believe that it is too late to communicate to your teen your desire for the teen to abstain from drugs and alcohol.

Here are eleven specific steps you can take with your teen in this area:

1. Offer a Rolex

I spoke at camp recently where I noticed a youth pastor wearing a Rolex watch. My curiosity got the better of me, so I asked him, "How in the world did you afford such a watch? And is your church hiring?"

"I could never afford a watch like this," he said. "I didn't buy it. My dad bought it for me when I graduated. He made a deal with me in high school that if I never took a drink or did drugs, he would buy me a Rolex watch when I graduated."

That's called the reward system. It can be one effective way of helping your teen through these years. Offer some sort of tangible, visible reward for embracing a lifestyle pleasing to God. It doesn't have to be a Rolex, but make sure it is something that is desirable enough to be valuable to your teen.

2. Get Your Teen Involved

One reason teens drink is to beat boredom. Encourage your teen to participate in sports, a hobby, church, a job, and after-school and weekend activities.

Ask your teen what he or she wants to do, since your teen will be most likely to participate in activities he or she is interested in.

3. Watch Your Example

One teen girl told me that her single mom used to come home from work each night and immediately pour herself a drink. Her mom never told her that it was okay to drink. But her mom did send the message to her that drinking helps take the edge off after a long day. How a person lives often speaks louder than words.

4. Don't Make Jokes

Avoid telling jokes and stories about drinking in such a way that conveys the message that alcohol or drug use is funny or glamorous. This trivializes the seriousness of the messages you want to convey about these subjects.

5. Trust Your Gut

Encourage your teen to trust instinct whenever he or she is in a situation that feels bad, such as when a new friend brings out drugs or alcohol. If the situation feels bad, it probably is bad. Your teen needs to leave.

6. Keep Your Teen from the Party

Teens usually know where the trouble is. They know who is into drinking and drugs and who isn't. Encourage them to avoid any party where they know or suspect there will be drugs and alcohol.

If your teen does go to parties, make sure your teen commits to agreements like the following:

- I won't go to a party thrown by anyone I or my parents don't know.
- I will only go to parties where there is adult supervision.
- I won't accept drinks from other people.

- I will open beverage containers myself.
- I will keep my drink with me at all times, even when I go to the bathroom.
- I won't share drinks.
- I won't drink from punch bowls or other open containers used in common.
- I won't drink anything that tastes or smells strange.

7. Warn About Drunk Driving

Remind your teen to never ride in a car with a driver who has been drinking. Let your teen know that if he or she is at a party or in a car with someone who has been drinking, your teen can call you from anywhere at any time. Communicate that you will come get your teen no matter the situation.

8. Don't Play Bartender

A teen girl told me that on prom night she had several friends over to her house after the dance. "My mom thought we would probably drink somewhere that night," the girl explained, "so she said we could come to my house and she would provide the alcohol."

Never serve alcohol to your teen or his or her friends. Sending such a message only encourages your teen to drink in other teens' homes with their parents. It is also illegal in most states to provide alcohol to minors who are not family members.

9. Lock Down Your Prescription Medicines

Putting your prescriptions under lock and key may seem extreme, but this may be a system you need to implement in your home to safeguard your teen.

Also, count your pills. Keep a note with your prescription of the date and time when you take some. This is work, but it will show your teen that you are serious about protecting him or her from danger.

10. Realize That Friends Do Matter

If your teen's friends drink, your teen is more likely to drink too. So encourage your teen to develop friendships with those who do not drink or use drugs. It is also imperative that you commit to knowing the parents of your teen's friends. Talk to your teen about the qualities in a friend that are truly important, such as honesty, integrity, and Christlikeness. (See chapter 13 for more about friendships.)

11. Let Yourself Be Known as the Freak

One dad told me that when his son was repeatedly encouraged to drink, he instructed his son, "Tell your friends, 'I can't drink. My dad is a freak. He will kill me if he finds out I was even around the stuff.'"

His son told them exactly that, and ever since, he hasn't been pressured. I have found that there are many teens who don't want to drink; they just need help coming up with a solid defense for why they shouldn't. Let your teen know it is okay to use you as the scapegoat.

Taking the Long View

Helping your teen draw the line with drugs and alcohol may not always be the easiest thing to do. But the long-term benefits of avoiding these harmful substances outweigh any difficulties you may encounter now. This is the battle we are in, so take up the Deep Breath Posture and fight.

Satan's side is trying to pull your teen away from God through the use of dangerous substances. But you can win the battle with God's help.

Praying Scripture for Your Teen

Father, You say in Your Word that we are to be filled with the Spirit, not be drunk with wine or any other substances. Please help me to help my teen in this area. Help my teen desire what is best in life. Help my teen gain the victory over the temptation of drugs and alcohol. Amen.

BASED ON EPHESIANS 5:18

13

YOUR TEEN'S FRIENDS

The Most Important Influencers

Close friendships matter at all ages and in every season of a person's life. But at no time does this become more apparent than during a person's teenage years. Your teen's friends are hugely important. My experience has shown that a teen's friends hold more influence over him or her than anybody else—more than parents, more than teachers, more than television or the media, more than youth pastors and mentors, more than anybody!

Recently I asked a group of teens to describe how important their friends are to them. Here's what a few of them had to say:

> I'd say my friends are very important to me. I just moved to this school this year, so I didn't know anyone at first. But after about three months, I started fitting in more. It was hard because all I ever wanted to do was e-mail my old friends in Iowa. (Faith, fourteen)

I guess you could say I switched "tribes" in January this year. I was hanging out with a group of friends that were really bringing me down. My youth pastor helped me see that who I hang out with affects what I become. So I made a hard decision and "switched lunch tables," as they say. At first my old friends all hated me. But now they just leave me alone. (Maya, fifteen)

I became a Christian this past summer at a Jose Zayas festival. Two friends from high school took me to it. I don't know much about Jesus yet, but I know I want to live for Christ. My friends are helping show me the way. My parents are divorced, and I live with my dad. He's not around much because he's always working. My friends are my family. They're always there for me. I spend most of my time over at their houses anyway. (Ryan, seventeen)

I wouldn't say I have real friends at school, merely acquaintances. I worked at a camp last summer as a counselor-in-training, and all my real friends are there. It's pretty tough going this year without any real friends. Mostly, all I feel like doing is sitting in my room talking to my friends from camp on the phone. My mom and dad don't really understand that I don't want to live in this town anymore. I'll be going to college next year, but it already feels like I've left home. (Joey, seventeen)

My friends and I do everything together. We're always together. We try and get the same classes together. We eat lunch in the same room. We've played on the same softball teams since we were in fifth grade. I'd say my friends are just about the most important thing to me in the whole world. (Michaela, fourteen)

Friends are powerful. Having the right friends matters to your teen. And your teen's having the right friends undoubtedly matters to you as a parent. Friends are the crucial link in building your teen up or tearing your teen down. Your teen spends hours and hours each week with people who greatly influence how your teen talks, thinks, acts, dresses, and generally does life. It is critical that your teen understands that who he or she spends time with will affect how the teen lives.

God makes it clear in Proverbs 13:20 that your teen needs to carefully consider his or her circle of influence: "He who walks with the wise grows wise, but a companion of fools suffers harm." That one verse is packed with many truths about choosing friends. First, there is a promise: "He who walks with the wise grows wise." God is saying that if your teen chooses to hang out with wise people, your teen will become wise. Second, there is a warning: "A companion of fools suffers harm." A foolish person is someone who knows the difference between right and wrong and yet consistently chooses to do wrong. God is saying that if your teen hangs out with such people, your teen will suffer.

Note that this passage of Scripture does not place the attention on *what* a person does. Instead, the focus is on *who* a person does things with. I realize that encouraging your teen to talk with you about friends may not be easy. But it is critical that you consistently keep tabs on your teen's friends.

It can be easy to want quality friends for your teen, but how does your teen make good friends if he or she doesn't yet have any? For your teen, it may not be as simple as walking up to a group of kids in the hallway and saying hello. Relationships during the teen years develop from a complex set of unspoken hierarchies, class systems, and cliques in your son or daughter's social circles. For a teen, friendships might be formed (or not formed) by being on a certain team, dressing a certain way, making certain grades, having a certain amount of money, or any number of other factors. What's a teen (or a parent) to do?

Advice for Choosing Wise Friends

Teens often ask me, "How do I choose good friends? How can I determine if my friends are wise and not foolish?" Let me offer several suggestions that can help you as a parent have a conversation with your teen about this topic and hopefully steer your teen away from the "foolish people" of the world.

Choosing Wise Friends Requires Honesty

Encourage your teen to honestly consider how his or her friends affect the way your teen lives, dresses, thinks, and acts. A wise friend will never ask your teen to do something that conflicts with the Bible. Your teen must consistently evaluate friendships by asking the tough questions.

One of the toughest yet most deeply important questions your teen needs to ask is, "Who is in control?" Let me explain what I mean.

In a friendship (or dating relationship), one person typically has more control in the relationship than the other. More times than not, teens make wrong choices because they fail to keep control. By "control," I mean that the other teen leads your teen or vice versa. In other words, if your teen is a natural leader and makes good choices, then others will be following your teen's positive example—not the other way around. It's important that your teen learn to keep control over situations and not be persuaded to make choices based upon what others desire or say is right.

Encourage your teen to consider the following questions about his or her friendships: *Do I have friends who...*

- *consistently tell me to do things I know are against God's will?*
- *make fun of me if I pray, read the Bible, or go to youth group or church?*
- *encourage me to lie to my parents and disobey their wishes?*
- *encourage me to watch movies, listen to music, or view Web sites that my parents and maybe I think are inappropriate?*

Choosing Wise Friends Requires Discretion

Communicate to your teen the importance of using discretion when it comes to choosing friends and making choices involving friends. Discretion is simply the freedom to choose. When your teen loses control over a situation, he or she loses freedom to make wise choices. Proverbs 2:11 says, "Discretion will protect you, and understanding will guard you."

I've seen a lot of teens make poor choices. And poor choices almost always lead to pain. Urge your teen to ask himself or herself one question: *Do my friends push me closer to, or pull me away from, God?* This question, if answered honestly, can be one of the easiest ways for teens to distinguish between healthy, God-honoring relationships and relationships that do not honor God.

If your teen is in a friendship that is proving harmful, it can be a tricky thing to have your teen end that friendship or even to put boundaries on it. As a parent, if you intervene here, it can easily cause friction. The place to start is always with your teen. Does your teen have the necessary strength to make the right choices without your intervention? If so, good. Part of the challenge here is to realize that if your teen ends a friendship, he or she may go through a season of solitude as a result. This will be difficult for your teen, and your sensitivity as a parent is highly important here.

If your teen does not want to end a harmful friendship on his or her own, here's where it's important to step in as a parent. Part of this is the Gritting Your Teeth Gesture ("whatever it takes is whatever it takes") fighting position we talked about in the first chapter.

In simple cases, it may involve drawing up a contract with your teen where the parameters of his or her friendship with this person (or group of people) is laid out on paper. You may need to set boundaries on when, where, and for how long your teen can interact with this person (or group).

In more serious cases, it might be necessary to establish stronger physical boundaries. I know one dad who actually had to nail the window to his daughter's room shut because she kept taking off in the middle of the night to meet up with her friends and get in trouble. No amount of conversation with her seemed to work. Nailing a window shut sounds extreme, but four years later the daughter is making much better choices. The tough parenting paid off.

What might it look like for you to establish stronger physical boundaries? You may need to have your teen change locations—that is, schools, sports teams, buses, and so on—to avoid contact with the harmful friend (or group of friends). You may need to more closely monitor cell phone and e-mail use or even take away your teen's cell phone or e-mail privileges for a while. Obviously, these are not easy things to implement in your home. But again, your call is to be the parent first, not a buddy to your teen.

Choosing Wise Friends Requires More Than Acceptance

Most teens gravitate toward a subculture of friends who accept them. We all do this to some extent. But what happens when the wrong group of friends accepts your teen? Or when acceptance becomes your teen's only criterion for friendships?

I am a strong proponent of teens' being choosy when it comes to their friends. I am not saying that your teen should look down on others or not associate with those who are not Christians. What I am saying is that it is imperative that your teen be wise in choosing to hang with the wise.

Work with your teen to help him or her discern which relationships are based upon wisdom and which aren't. An important point to consider is intent. Jesus hung out with people from all walks of life, but He didn't hang out with people just to have a good time. His intent in every relationship was to point His friends—and enemies—to His Father. Does your teen have this same intent when it comes to friendships?

Even with the best of intentions, not every teen is spiritually mature enough to undertake such a responsibility. You, as a parent, can help your teen discern whether he or she is ready for such a challenge.

Choosing Wise Friends Requires Maintaining Accountability

Jesus demonstrated accountability throughout His three-year ministry. He assembled a group and did life with them. Encourage your teen to do the same.

Be proactive in this investment. Offer to drive your teen to meet with others. Give your teen money for a latte. Stock the fridge, order a pizza (or ten), and give your teen and his or her friends the green light each week to hang out in your living room while they encourage one another to go deeper in their walks with God. (I can't think of many investments with greater returns.)

Encouraging your teen to get involved in accountability with others will impact your teen on many levels. Accountability will let your teen know that he or she is not alone in the battle with the Enemy. It will invigorate your teen to know there are others praying for him or her. It will empower your teen to celebrate triumphant moments in his or her spiritual journey.

I know a group of teens that meets every Sunday night at Starbucks here in Nashville just to talk about life, encourage one another, read the Scriptures, pray, and celebrate one another's spiritual victories. How cool it is that these teens take their walk with God so seriously that they understand the importance of remaining accountable to one another!

Choosing Wise Friends Requires Making No Compromise

If your teen's friends consistently pull him or her away from living a God-centered life, then it may be time for your teen to make new friends. This may be easier said than done, but helping your teen to understand the warning of Proverbs 13:20 is crucial. God did not say that harm *might* result from choosing unwise friends. He spoke clearly: a companion of fools *will* suffer harm.

Parent, I encourage you to consistently learn about your teen's friends. Ask yourself questions such as these:

- *Who is my teen's best friend?*
- *Do I know who my teen spends most of his or her time with?*
- *Who does my teen talk to on the phone?*
- *Who is my teen dating (or interested in dating)?*
- *Who are the five most important friends in my teen's life?*

Getting to know your teen's friends most likely will not be as simple as asking your teen who he or she spends time with. Even if your teen begins to name names, it is about more than simply knowing a name. You need to know the people. As a connected parent, you need to know the beliefs, habits, and spiritual maturity of the people your teen considers friends. The best way to know your teen's friends is to spend time with them.

One father recently told me, "I just turned our basement into a cool hangout for Reed, my son. We put a fridge down there, got a big TV, and purchased a pool table. This was a costly decision but one my wife and I hope will pay off."

This dad went on to explain that his son had been hanging out with some new friends at school and he had been trying to figure out a way to keep tabs on these new friends. His hope was that his son would bring his friends over to the house more often. Good idea.

As with this dad's experience, the desire to stay connected to your teen may involve spending money. Whether you need to buy a Ping-Pong table or simply throw a pizza party after the game on Friday night, I encourage you to invest what it takes to become better educated about your teen's friends.

Knowing your teen's friends includes knowing their parents. If your teen is not in your home, then he or she is most likely in the home of another parent. This means that not only are your teen's friends influencing your teen, but also *the parents of your teen's friends* are influencing your teen. Unless you strap a mobile camera to your teen's forehead, which I don't recommend, you must find another way to be in the know.

You may find that you are the only parent making an effort to better know other parents. That is okay. Again, rely on the Gritting Your Teeth Gesture: whatever it takes is whatever it takes. But usually, other parents will respond when you make the first effort to be connected.

One mom recently told me that she started walking with several moms of her teen's friends. This provided her an excellent opportunity to better know them and to express her concerns and values.

Better Friends, Better Life

The subject of friends is an area where entering the fight becomes critical. The wrong friends can impact your teen in very harmful ways. The right friends can make all the difference during these important years.

Friendships are seldom easy to either make or break. Trusting in your Ultimate Power Stance, pray that God will provide a window of opportunity for you to consistently engage in conversations with your teen about friendships.

Your teen's friendships do matter. As you consistently encourage your teen in this area, your teen will know that you care, even if he or she doesn't always agree with you. The reward will come in the end. Let's take the matter to the Lord in prayer right now.

Praying Scripture for Your Teen

O God, You say in Your Word that we should guard clear thinking and common sense. Help my teen do that with friendships. Help my teen to have friends who lead my teen closer to God. Help my teen to lead others closer to God. In Jesus's name. Amen.

BASED ON PROVERBS 3:21 (MSG)

14

THE SECRETS TEENS KEEP

A Brief Guide to the Root Issue

When I was in high school, I was shy and lacked confidence. I was skinny and had a lot of pimples. When I looked in the mirror, I hated myself. In fact, for a while I hated myself so much that I actually wanted to die.

I carried that secret around for quite some time. I never told anybody about it, but inside I felt miserable. When I finally told my parents how I was feeling, they were able to help me.

We all have secrets. We all have things about ourselves that we try to hide from others. That's just the way it is. We don't want to be embarrassed, or we don't want people to see how vulnerable we are or how much we're hurting.

Over the years, I've talked to a lot of teens who have secrets—secrets about their pasts, their bodies, their pain, their families, their addictions, and tons more. Not every teen has the same secrets, of course. But since this is a book with a limited number of pages, in this chapter I want to talk about a few of the main secrets that I see teens keeping.

Why talk about secrets? Because living a lie ultimately destroys us, those around us, and the relationships we care about most. Proverbs 28:13 says, "He who conceals his sins does not prosper, but whoever confesses and renounces them finds mercy." This means that when your teen is hiding a secret from you—or from anyone else—that secret has power over his or her life.

Sin thrives in darkness. But when that sin is uncovered, it has no place to run. Whenever we expose secrets, we take away the power they have over us and our families.

Think of this chapter as an invitation to let Jesus Christ lead you in a good direction. It's not an exhaustive treatment on each type of secret. Rather, this chapter is about helping your teen be real and be healed. If your teen has a harmful secret in his or her life, God can help your teen change directions. Just the tiniest bit of faith can transform a desperate situation into an opportunity for God's amazing grace to come in, cleanse, and restore. God can make right the things in your family's life that seem impossible to repair.

Common Teen Secrets

You need to use your Open Book Motion here. Some of what you will learn about present-day teen culture may be sad and scary for you. But let's go ahead and take a look at some of the most prevalent secrets I see in teens' lives today.

Teens Are Cutting Themselves

At a recent event where I spoke, a teen named Jamie rolled up the bottom of her pants to show me scars on her legs. "I've been cutting myself for two years," she said. "It started in junior high. I never felt like I was as good as my older sister. She was like a rock star at our school. Perfect grades, class president, a softball and volleyball athlete. Everybody knew her and loved her." By now, Jamie was crying uncontrollably. "Who could ever compete with someone that perfect?" she said.

Jamie's self-mutilation might have been a secret, but her pain wasn't. The sadness in her eyes gave her away. Anybody paying attention would have seen how lonely, broken, and insecure she was just by looking at her.

To some people, cutting sounds crazy. Why would anyone want to hurt himself or herself like that? As parents, we might find it hard to understand the motivation for such behavior. But the fact is, there's a lot of hurt inside some teens, and it just keeps building until they feel like they can't stand it anymore. Some teens cut to cope. Some cut to get attention. Others do it at first out of curiosity or as an escape from emotional pain.

Teens Have Eating Disorders

Another teen, Rebecca, approached me after an event and asked if we could talk. By outward appearances, she had all a teen could want: blonde hair, popularity, a wealthy family. But from the outside looking in, you never would have known how much self-hatred she was hiding. And it had come to affect her relationship with food.

The first time Rebecca made herself throw up was a few weeks before her junior prom. "It was disgusting for me to think about making myself vomit," she told me. "But I convinced myself that the results I saw in the mirror would be worth it." Rebecca first read about purging online and thought it would be the perfect way to shed a few pounds before the big dance. A few days later and a few pounds lighter, Rebecca was convinced she'd found the perfect way to diet. She was also convinced she had the whole thing under control.

Teens live in a world that puts a lot of pressure on them to be physically flawless. That pressure can lead to anorexia, bulimia, and even overeating. Rebecca's problem started innocently enough—she just wanted to be a little thinner for prom. She wanted to be liked, to be a little closer to perfect. Those feelings seem benign, but teens can become obsessed with getting approval from the people around them. The damage to their bodies and psyches can be severe.

Teens Are Choking Themselves

There's a horrible game in town. It's been around for years in various forms, but it's always dangerous. Recently, the brother of a close friend of mine died while playing it. Today the game goes by various aliases—the Choking Game, the Pass-Out Game, the Funky Chicken, the Space Cowboy Game, and simply Gasp. A recent survey noted that 75 percent of kids ages nine to sixteen "know how the game is played or have played it themselves," but only 25 percent of parents know about the game.[1]

The game is actually a form of self-asphyxiation in which a teen cuts off the oxygen to his or her brain using a belt, a rope, a sheet, a scarf, or hands. When the teen feels as though he or she will faint, the teen releases the restraint from around the throat. Blood then rushes to the brain, creating a high. Fainting can easily occur if the restraint is not removed quickly enough. The obvious danger is that if a teen passes out before releasing the restraint, the teen is strangled.

Teens often get off on this dangerous buzz with others at parties, at school, or at home alone. Some students, usually teen boys, use this

---

1. The DB Foundation, "'The Choking Game': Advocating Education of the Dangers," ChokingGame.net, www.chokinggame.net/?gclid=CPPGosHP_JMCFScuagodYy5xWg (accessed June 18, 2008).

game while masturbating, since it is said to heighten their sense of sexual pleasure.

What the practitioners of this game seldom realize is that this activity is also extremely dangerous. It can...

- kill brain cells
- cause bruising
- cause retinal hemorrhaging
- cause stroke
- cause seizures
- lead to death

Signs your teen may be playing the game include the following:

- marks on the side of neck
- a flushed face
- intense headaches
- unusual demands for privacy
- wear marks on furniture such as bunk beds or closet rods
- a rope, a belt, or something else of that sort continually lying around

The choking game reminds us that the costs of letting teens' secrets remain secret are far higher than any caring parent is willing to pay.

Keeping the Focus for Your Teen

We could talk about so many more secrets in this book: depression, issues with self-worth, problems with grades, and problems with peer pressure, to name only a few. But I'd rather bring the focus back around to God.

The ultimate solution to any harmful secret your teen is keeping within himself or herself is to point your teen to the Lord. When your teen is pointed in the right direction, he or she will find the solution with your help as a parent. The key is to keep talking, to keep asking your teen questions, and to help your teen see the answers in God's Word.

God knows exactly what's happening in your teen's heart and life. Just look at what the Bible says: "Praise be to the Lord, to God our Savior, who daily bears our burdens" (Psalm 68:19). And "Come to me, all you who are weary and burdened, and I will give you rest" (Matthew 11:28). When the Bible says that God bears your teen's burdens, it means it.

Here's the battle you're in: Satan wants your teen to believe that his or her secret is something to feel ashamed of. He wants your teen to believe that he or she should never talk to anyone about it, particularly you and your spouse. He wants to convince your teen that no one will understand him or her.

Don't buy it. And encourage your teen not to buy the lies either. If your teen has secrets, your teen is not messed up, weird, dysfunctional, or a freak. We all have secrets. The difference between those who overcome their problems and those who stay trapped by them is belief— belief that God's truth is stronger than Satan's lies.

If you suspect that your teen's secrets are harming him or her, start by encouraging your teen with the truth that God knows all secrets (see Psalm 44:21). Your teen's story is no surprise to Him. God sees your teen as he or she truly is, and God loves your teen. God wants your teen to become all that He intends.

After pointing your teen to God, the next thing is to confirm that the activity is happening. If your communication channel is open with your teen, then he or she may come out and tell you the truth if asked. But one secret typically leads to another, and your teen may not give you a straight answer.

Let your teen know that taking the first step—admitting that a problem exists—is the hardest. But once people open up about their secrets, they often feel a great sense of relief. If you suspect a problem but your teen is unwilling to talk, suggest that he or she choose someone else to talk to first—a school counselor, a coach, a youth pastor, a doctor, or a nurse. Or your teen may want to write you a note or letter if the topic feels too difficult to bring up in person.

Bringing the secret out into the open is important. But beyond that, help your teen identify the trouble that's triggering the secret. Harmful outward behaviors are typically a way of reacting to inner emotional tension or pain. Try to help your teen figure out what feelings or situations are causing the secret behavior. Is it anger? Pressure to be perfect? Relationship trouble? A painful loss or trauma? Criticism or mistreatment? Many teens will have trouble figuring this part out on their own. This is where a trusted, Christian mental-health professional can be helpful.

It takes a while for most teens to sort through strong feelings and learn better ways of coping with life's stresses. This is where the Deep Breath Posture fighting position comes into play. Be willing to walk through a season of difficulty with your teen. And remember, there is hope. God can make all things beautiful in His time.

God's Call to Faithfulness

Obviously, this chapter doesn't take an exhaustive approach to issues like cutting and purging, but I wanted to write it to offer a broad view of where to turn, no matter what you're facing with your teen. Whatever secret your teen is keeping, help your teen to honestly face the secret and then begin to talk to others about it. When talking begins, secrets lose their power, and help and healing can begin.

God understands exactly where your teen is. God can use even the darkest times in your teen's life to complete His plan. Nothing is so bad that He can't make it into something good.

It's always easier to observe pain at a distance than it is to roll up our sleeves and step forward to help. But as parents committed to the best for our teens, we need to be proactive in helping our teens when they're in need. This is our call, our invitation, and our privilege. God has brought us to this place for such a time as this (see Esther 4:14).

Let's adopt the Ultimate Power Stance and do some praying about this area right now.

Praying Scripture for Your Teen

O God, You say in Your Word that hope does not disappoint us, because You've poured out Your love into our hearts by the Holy Spirit, whom You have given us. Right now, I want to pray a prayer of hope for my teen. Help my teen talk about what's truly happening in his or her life. Help my teen not be held hostage by secrets. Help my teen, by Your love and power, to be all You want my teen to be. Amen.

BASED ON ROMANS 5:5

PART 3

HOPE AHEAD FOR EVERY FAMILY

15

GOING PUBLIC WITH GOD

Helping Your Teen Develop and Share Faith

Have you heard the story about the two rednecks Duke and Luke? A field separated their homes. One morning Luke noticed his neighbor was standing in the middle of the field. Luke put on his John Deere ball cap, grabbed a pinch of dip, and walked across the field to Duke.

"Whatcha doing standing out here in this field so early in the morning?" Luke asked.

"Why, I'm hopin' to win the Nobel Prize!" exclaimed Duke.

"Duke, jest how you think you're gonna win the Nobel Prize?"

"Well, Luke," said Duke confidently, "everyone knows that to win the Nobel Prize you gotta be out standing in your field."

I know—a ridiculous joke. But it shows that right from the beginning, someone can be ill-equipped to succeed. No matter how long Duke persevered in that field, he was never going to be a recipient of the Nobel Prize. All he would ever get from standing in that field was a sunburn. Purpose in life, true purpose, is about much more than winning earthly acclaim or treasure.

I am confident that Jesus fully understood this truth. From the virgin birth to the empty tomb and ultimately to His return to heaven, Jesus had one purpose—to go public with God. Every day Jesus's life exemplified this purpose. His final charge to His followers, and to all Christ-followers, clearly defined the true purpose for which we, too, are called to live: "Go and make disciples of all nations" (Matthew 28:19).

This is the call on your teen's life—to go public with God!

Building a Relationship with God

When teens desire to share truth with a world desperate for God's love, it often gives them a hope they have never felt before. Christ's commission fuels their lives and provides a greater purpose to the choices they make about the paths they walk down. The call is to be like Jesus to the world—to undertake the ministry of Jesus Christ and lead others closer to God.

Teens who accept this challenge are often excited and confident to follow Christ's command. But I also meet a lot of teens who feel insecure and ill-equipped to put feet to a desire of sharing Jesus with others. And this is where you, as a parent, come in. You can be your teen's coach, adviser, and encourager as he or she seeks to go public with faith.

The first part of this task may not be what you think. The first part of helping your teen be a bold Christian in the world is encouraging your teen to develop his or her *own* relationship with God.

Your teen does not have to be a biblical expert or attend seminary. What's important is that he or she takes the necessary steps to know God better. When this happens, your teen will step out fearlessly as he or she chooses to go public with Him.

The problem is that in this ATM, digital download, high-speed DSL, drive-through, texting way of life, teens are looking for the quick and easy, even when it comes to their walk with God. Developing a committed relationship with Jesus, though, is something that takes time. So you must help your teen commit to spending time reading Scripture, talking to God, and listening to His direction.

Time in the Word

To go public with God, your teen needs a biblical foundation upon which he or she can build. The Bible is spiritual sustenance. But the sad reality is that many teens spend little, if any, time reading the Bible. They see the Bible as archaic, irrelevant, or hard to understand.

So how can a parent help a teen see God's Word in a fresh way and as making a difference in real life?

Choose a modern Bible version. If your teen has spent little to no time reading the Bible, getting a new version could be a first step in the right direction. Take your teen to a Christian bookstore and browse through different versions of the Bible. One that I especially enjoy reading is The Message. The creator of this paraphrase of the Bible writes in a way that teens and adults can easily relate to. The New International Version and Holman Christian Standard Bible are two translations I also recommend.

Not every teen needs to be introduced to the Bible. One teen told me, "I have the Bible on my laptop. I often use it when talking with friends." Another teen told me she has it on her cell phone. How cool!

The idea here is to do what it takes to help your teen connect with God's Word. Buying your teen a new Bible, whether it's made of paper or pixels, will not guarantee that he or she will commit to consistently plugging in to the Word or applying it to life. But creatively encouraging your teen to apply Scripture to life, while also spending consistent time in the Word yourself, will send a strong message to your teen about what's important.

Create a reading plan. If your teen hasn't spent much time in the Word, here is a simple application that could be the jump-start he or she needs to spend consistent time with God. My suggested reading plan is to read one chapter, the same chapter, every day for one week. Then, when the next week comes around, read another chapter.

I don't know about you, but there are times when I read the Bible and then immediately forget what I've read. Going back and reading the same chapter each day for one week helps me and will help your teen absorb the truth of Scripture.

Of course, there will be days when your teen chooses not to read the Bible. Be careful not to push your teen too hard or criticize him or her for not reading the Bible every day, since this may prompt your teen to ignore Scripture altogether. The key word is consistency. Continue to encourage your teen about spending time in the Word more consistently, even if it's not absolutely every day, but don't force the issue. Help your teen find a way that works for him or her.

Commit to living by the Word. Psalm 119:9–11—a great passage for teens—says,

> How can a young man keep his way pure?
> > By living according to your word.
> I seek you with all my heart;
> > do not let me stray from your commands.
> I have hidden your word in my heart
> > that I might not sin against you.

Psalm 119 makes it clear that by spending time in the Word, a person will gain knowledge, develop a greater understanding of who God is, and be able to stand for what is right, no matter the circumstance.

I often encourage teens to turn to specific scriptures that deal with everyday issues they struggle with, such as temptation, guilt, and choices. Why don't you try that approach? A reference work like a concordance or a topical Bible can be a big help in finding verses that relate to the issues your teen is facing. Or urge your teen to use an online resource like BibleGateway.com.

Time in Prayer

As your teen commits time to reading the Bible, prayer will hopefully become a greater part of his or her life as well. First Thessalonians 5:17 says, "Pray all the time" (MSG). Explain to your teen the reality of this verse. Your teen really can pray *any*time!

It is also important to help your teen realize the many different ways he or she can pray. Doing the same thing over and over might get old, especially to a teen. And anyway, prayer is not about having a once-a-day ritual during devotions, nor is it merely about thanking God before eating a meal. It is about an all-consuming lifestyle of communication with God, not only anytime but also anywhere and about anything. A father of three gives this great idea on creative prayer:

> During our family devo times, we recently started encouraging
> our teens to e-mail their prayers to God. We came up with a
> bogus address, and each teen would take five minutes at the end
> of their devotional time to send an e-mail to God. I think they
> began to put a lot more thought into their words, and it made
> prayer more real and intimate for them, like they were actually

communicating with a friend. The neat thing is that five minutes eventually became six, and then eight, and then ten.

God desires for your teen to be honest, sincere, and real with Him. Prayer offers your teen the opportunity to do just that.

Time Spent Listening

Getting to know God requires not only talking with Him but also listening to Him. This is one area where Satan puts in overtime in his fight to get us to buy lies. One such lie? "You can't hear God. It's ridiculous to even imagine that God would actually talk to you!"

One teen wrote me to say, "Last week at camp you talked about hearing the voice of God. Jeffrey, I've been a Christian for almost ten years, and I don't think I've ever heard God's voice."

My response was, "Neither have I—audibly, anyway. But I know He communicates with me."

The question is not, does God speak? The question is, do we choose to listen? As parents, we have to teach our children how to train their ears to listen to God speaking to us through the Holy Spirit.

What does God's voice sound like? For one thing, it can be a pang of conscience. Your teen has probably been faced with a temptation to take a drink of alcohol, smoke pot, gossip, or cheat on a test. In that tempting moment, the teen probably stopped to consider the choice. And even if only for a moment, your teen felt something that reminded him or her of the right thing to do. That feeling wasn't *just* a feeling. That was the Holy Spirit speaking to your teen. His words may not be audible, but His truths are always loud and clear.

Another important factor in helping your teen listen to the voice of God is addressed in Proverbs 3:5–6:

Trust in the LORD with all your heart
> and lean not on your own understanding;
in all your ways acknowledge him,
> and he will make your paths straight.

What we learn here is that an integral part of your teen's hearing the voice of God is trusting Him with every area of life. Many teens miss this point. They want God only when they need Him. They want God when their world is falling apart. They want God when friends have hurt them, when they have a major test, or when that huge pimple appears on the morning of prom. Yet they often fail to trust God and "acknowledge him" in all of their ways during the good days of life.

Your role here is to help your teen see you as an example of one who trusts God with all your heart, so that your teen will learn to do the same.

What It Looks Like to Go Public

Spending time in the Word, spending time in prayer, and spending time listening to God are three vital steps to being prepared to go public with Him. But then what happens? It's time to actually live and speak for Jesus in a way that others will recognize. And that's where it all gets very real.

At the beginning of my senior year of high school, I committed to going public with God on my campus. God took my commitment seriously. But my first assignment didn't turn out as I planned.

A kid named Eric and I had been enemies since junior high. I often wondered why Eric didn't like me. One day he told me straight out that it was because I was a Christian. So when I heard God tell me that He wanted me to talk to Eric about what it means to be a Christian, I assumed God was mistaken. But God wasn't joking. God really wanted me to talk with Eric about my faith.

I ignored God's request for four months, and I was miserable because of it. Finally I called Eric and gave the speech of my life. At the end of the call, just after giving myself a high-five for a job well done, I asked Eric if he would like to pray and receive Jesus into his life.

Eric politely said no, then hung up.

"What? You have *got* to be kidding, God," I said to Him. "It wasn't supposed to work this way." I was so disappointed. I felt like I had done what God asked me to, but He hadn't come through for me. I was mad at God.

It took me a while, but I learned a lot through that experience. I learned that there's more to sharing my faith than the outcome. I learned that, regardless of how others respond, I have a responsibility to go public with God, even though I may not like the person I'm to go public before or the outcome of my presentation.

Talking with another person about Jesus is serious stuff. As your teen commits to getting serious about living for Christ, get ready, because along with this commitment comes the responsibility to share Christ with others. The outcome, though, is always up to the Holy Spirit.

Ready to "Go"

So let's say your teen is ready to "go and make disciples" in his or her own world. How can your teen go about this? How can you help?

In addition to sharing whatever insights you've gained through your own witnessing experiences, here are a few practical steps to help your teen develop a plan for going public.

1. Start by explaining the principle Jesus outlines in Matthew 28:18–20.

2. Help your teen write out his or her story of faith. A personal testimony answers these questions:
    - Who is God to you?
    - What did God do for you?
    - How has God changed you?

    By the way, your teen doesn't have to have a story of running away from home, attempting suicide, or robbing a bank for his or her testimony to be worth telling. Your teen's story is an incredible one due to the simple fact that he or she was once destined for hell and now is not.

3. Encourage your teen to make a list of people in his or her life with whom the teen desires to go public. Your teen then can start praying for God to provide opportunities to share Jesus with these people.

4. Help your teen prepare what he or she is going to say. The teen can use questions like these:
    - "Do you believe in God?"
    - "What do you believe about God?"
    - "What confuses you the most about God?"
    - "Have you ever prayed to give your life to Jesus? Would you like to right now?"

    The teen should also be familiar with the plan of salvation, or the biblical rationale for trusting in Jesus. Perhaps you could role-play an evangelistic conversation with your teen, playing the part of the unbeliever.

5. As your teen makes attempts to go public with his or her faith, check in regularly with what's happening, and provide

THE PLAN OF SALVATION

There are many who believe that living a good life will get them into heaven. But Jesus said, "I am the way and the truth and the life. No one comes to the Father except through me" (John 14:6). A personal relationship with Jesus is the only way to God and the only way into heaven. Here's an outline your teen can use to explain to someone else how to have that kind of personal relationship.

1. Recognize God's Plan

God loves you and has a plan for your life. The Bible says, "God so loved the world that he gave his one and only Son, that whoever believes in him shall not perish but have eternal life" (John 3:16). This is God's plan for your life, that you spend an eternity with Him in heaven.

2. Realize the Problem

Every human chooses to disobey God and do his or her own thing. The result is that we are separated from God, because He is perfect and we are sinners. The Bible says, "All have sinned and fall short of the glory of God" (Romans 3:23).

3. Respond to God's Remedy

Because God loves you so much, He sent His Son to bridge the gap between you and Him that exists because of your wrong choices. God's Son, Jesus Christ, paid the penalty for your sins when He died on the cross and rose from the grave. The Bible says, "God demonstrates his own love for us in this: While we were still sinners, Christ died for us" (Romans 5:8).

4. Receive Christ

By asking Christ to come into your life, you cross the bridge into God's family. God then forgives you and offers you a relationship with Him and the privilege of spending eternity with Him in heaven one day. The Bible says, "To all who received him, to those who believed in his name, he gave the right to become children of God" (John 1:12).

How do you receive Christ? You can stop right now, wherever you are, and pray a prayer such as this one:

Dear Jesus, I realize that I am a sinner and I need your forgiveness. I believe that You are the Son of God and that You died for me. I want to give my life over to You by asking You to forgive me of all my past mistakes. I now invite You into my life to save me and change me and be the Lord of my life. Thank You for loving me. Amen.

ongoing encouragement. Remind your teen that while sometimes one conversation is all it takes to bring a friend to Jesus, at other times extended prayer and patience will be needed.

6. Commit to praying these things for your teen. Pray that:
   • God will provide the opportunity.
   • God will provide the boldness.
   • God will provide the words.
   • God will bring honor to Himself through the outcome.

Killing the Fear

I meet teens everywhere who have no fear when given the opportunity to climb onto a stage and morph into a rock star. Other teens are fearless on an athletic field. So why is it that many teens act fearful when given the opportunity to share Jesus with others?

It is because many have never been consistently encouraged to share their faith. Also, some teens don't realize that going public is not about carrying a Bible around at school or quoting Scripture. It's about a life surrendered. It's about embracing God's ways over the world's. It's about staring the Enemy in the face with the same intensity you take into the game each Friday night and declaring war for the sake of the kingdom of God.

One teen said to me, "But what if someone asks me a question about God or the Bible that I don't know how to answer? Shouldn't I hold off on talking to others about Jesus until I know everything about the Bible?"

Fear over what your teen doesn't know is a tactic Satan loves to use in battle against your teen. But encourage your teen to be honest when someone asks a question he or she doesn't know the answer to. Your teen can simply tell the friend that he or she will find an answer. Let your teen know that you or a pastor would love to help in that process.

Witnessing may seem overwhelming at first. But as your teen commits to time in the Word, time in prayer, and time listening to God, God will reveal Himself to your teen in amazing ways. Fear will be replaced with fearlessness. And your teen's faith journey will become a story he or she can't wait to share with others.

Praying Scripture for Your Teen

God, You say in Your Word to always be prepared to give an answer to everyone who asks us to give the reason for the hope that we have. Help my teen (and me) to do that. You say that you have not given us a spirit of fear, but of power and love and self-discipline. Help us never to be afraid in going public with our faith in You. Amen.

BASED ON 1 PETER 3:15 AND 2 TIMOTHY 1:7–8

16

COME ALL THE WAY

Helping Your Teen Live Life to the Full

Several years ago I was speaking at a camp in Wisconsin and got the opportunity to go caving with a guide and a group of teens. Caving (or spelunking) is an incredible rush. With lighted helmets, we began going deeper and deeper into this cave. The further we descended, the colder it became, and little by little teens began to turn and make their way back to the surface. I continued on for several hours, until our group had dwindled to just me, two teen boys, and our guide, Ryan.

The further we went, the more difficult it became. The walls tightened in around us. We went from walking to kneeling to crawling to sliding on our bellies.

Eventually we reached our destination: the door to what was known as the Mud Room. Our guide had been preparing us for what he described as "the coolest thing underground" he had ever seen. This was a room approximately twelve by fifteen feet in size. The walls, the ceiling, the floor—everything was completely layered with thick, gooey mud.

There was only one problem—the door to the Mud Room was an incredibly tight squeeze. Ryan shimmied through, expecting the rest of us to follow. But none of us moved. The needle's eye through which Ryan had just passed was so small that each of us realized it was going to take some tricky maneuvering to slide our bodies safely through to the other side. After much hesitation, I decided to throw in the towel. I hollered down the hole to Ryan that we would not be joining him.

Ryan hollered back to me something I will not soon forget. As he answered, his voice echoed through the chambers of the cave, "Jeffrey, you can't come this far and not come all the way."

I thought about it and realized Ryan was right, so I took a deep breath and descended into the hole, as did the two teen guys. I am so glad we did. Ryan was right. The Mud Room was exactly that—a small, air-filled cavity in the midst of a dense mud bog. In some ways the room felt unsafe, but that Mud Room had been there without incident for a long, long time. It's amazing to think such strange and wondrous places exist on earth.

Here's what has stuck with me for all these years. It was Ryan's statement: "You can't come this far and not come all the way." That's a great line when it comes to parenting. Kids need us to *come all the way* in our relationship with them. That means we need to be willing to grit our teeth and do whatever it takes to guide our kids on their expedition through the teen years.

Recently I talked with a group of parents whose children are now in college or have graduated high school and entered careers. They described how their job as parents isn't fully over yet, even now that their kids have become adults. Parents will always remain parents. But all of them expressed satisfaction to one degree or another in knowing that their kids had made it through the teenage years. Some of the parents had experienced a rocky season during those years, while other families had made it through the battle relatively unscathed. Regardless, I asked them to write down some words of wisdom "from the other side." Here's what a few of them had to say:

When children rebel during the teenage years, you often hear things like, "Well, it was the parents' fault." But that's not always the case. It's true that parents play an incredible part in this battle, yet God gives all people free will, including teenagers.

We have two children, a boy and a girl, and always raised both of them to love and honor God. The girl made it through the teen years just fine. The boy had a much rougher go of it. (We are now raising our first grandchild because of one of his decisions.)

I think it's important to know that even if you do everything as well as you can as parents, your children might still make poor choices. During some of our harder years, we found great comfort in Proverbs 22:6: "Train a child in the way he should go, and when he is old he will not turn from it." (Steve and Mary-Catherine)

I'd say we went through about eight months of absolute agony with our middle daughter, Stephanie. We tried everything we could think of. At least once every day we had a full-blown heated conversation. We had contracts, agreements, lists, charts; we took her to counseling; we prayed nonstop.

Somehow all the hard work must have paid off, because she has stopped drinking now, is (mostly) back on track with the

Lord, and is through her second year in arts school. (Ben and Larken)

We have five children (although the youngest died as an infant). Three of our kids seemed to just experience the normal ups and downs of teenage years. Two are married now and are starting families of their own. One just graduated from college.

Our youngest had a hard time, particularly his junior and senior years, when my husband did his first tour in Iraq for sixteen months. Aaron just seemed to fall apart then. I didn't know what to do. I think that I just gave up for part of that time. But Aaron made friends with a Young Life sponsor at his school, which was about the only positive influence Aaron would allow into his life during those years.

Aaron is doing much better now. When he graduated high school, he went into the military and is a cook now at a Marine base near Mosul. I know it can be hard in the military, but when he writes and calls home, his tone is still tender to things of the Lord. We're really proud of Aaron and how far he's come. (Jenn and Steve)

Did you hear the hope in those stories? Though the path through the teen years can often be challenging, the hard work almost always pays off in the end. That can be consolation right now in the midst of the fight.

Your teen is exploring new territory every day. Though the terrain before him or her may seem safe, lurking around every dark corner is the Enemy waiting for the opportunity to lead your teen astray. Though your teen may not always request your guidance, he or she desperately needs it. Your teen is relying on you to help him or her finish the journey strong. That's what this book has been all about. And I realize there's a lot of content in this book that will take a while to sort through and implement into your life. This is okay. Parenting is not a sprint. The journey both you and your teen are on is an ongoing one. So assume your Deep Breath Posture.

A Parent Who Comes All the Way—How to "Be"

As you process all that we have discussed in this book, I want to offer a few final thoughts that can help you *come all the way* with your teen as you fight for your teen's best.

Be Forewarned

As you complete this book, Satan will begin to throw everything he has at you to convince you that what you've read isn't necessary for your teen. Satan will not rest, because he knows that what you've read in these pages is truth. He wants you to forget it as quickly as you read it.

Pray for protection over yourself and your family. Write down the passage below and put it someplace where you can see it often as a reminder to pray for your family:

> The LORD will keep you from all harm—
>   he will watch over your life;
> the LORD will watch over your coming and going
>   both now and forevermore. (Psalm 121:7–8)

Be a Pray-er

I am fully convinced that the key to it all is prayer. I will ask you again, if you are not spending time praying for your teen, who is? In this battle, your greatest defense is to pray daily for your teen. It is your Ultimate Power Stance. A strong way to let your teen know that he or she is extremely important to you is to let your teen know that you pray for him or her every day.

Be Bold

As you continue to strive to *come all the way* for your teen, remember that your teen is counting on you to do everything within your power and ability to protect him or her from getting destroyed. Fighting the good fight is not for wimps. Your goal must be to arm yourself for battle and be ready to do whatever is necessary to guide and guard your teen through these entangling years. Your teen needs you to be a parent willing to rebel against the mainstream and take bold steps toward staying connected with him or her on a level that radically impacts your teen's life.

Is this not the bold step that Christ took for us? The Son of God, Jesus, stepped out of heaven and stepped into our lives on earth because He understood what it meant to take extreme measures to connect with those He loves.

A bold parent must be willing to have his or her heart tattooed with the Gritting Your Teeth Gesture motto: "Whatever it takes is whatever it takes."

Be Worthy of Honor

Each of us must ask, *Am I a parent worthy of honor?* I am not saying that if you have *not* been such a parent, a child has the right to dishonor you. The fifth commandment (Deuteronomy 5:16) does not say, "Honor your father and mother as long as they deserve it." God's commandment is clear and distinct: "Honor your father and your mother," period!

I believe that years from now my children will consistently choose to honor me if I have adequately followed God's commands to "be careful, and watch yourselves closely so that you do not forget the things your eyes have seen or let them slip from your heart as long as you live. Teach them to your children and to their children after them" (Deuteronomy 4:9).

It is my hope that you will hold on to the biblical truths reflected in this book so that your teen doesn't simply honor you out of duty. Rather, may your teen choose to do so out of reverence for God and respect for your life example.

Be Knowledgeable About Your Teen

The more you know about your teen, the more equipped you are to lead your teen. Look for creative ways to educate yourself more on what is important to your teen, what your teen's struggles are, what your teen finds challenging about God, how your teen desires to pursue God daily, and more. Consider sending your teen an e-mail with questions such as these:

- Who is your favorite band?
- If you could change one thing about your body, what would it be?
- If you could plan the perfect vacation, where would you go and what would you do?
- What is the one question you would ask God if you had the chance?
- What three things confuse or frustrate you the most about God?
- If you could change one thing about our relationship, what would you change?

Be Educated About Education

I am convinced that the public-school campuses of America are the number one mission field in our nation today. Which means that your teen is literally entering a mission field—and a war zone—every day.

What can you do? You can use the Open Book Motion and take steps to know what is being taught to your teen. Most special classes, such as the sex education classes described in an earlier chapter, can be attended by your teen only with your consent as a parent. Do not simply sign your name to the dotted line, no matter the course description. Call the school. Or even better, visit the classroom, talk with the teacher, and request a copy of the curriculum from which your teen will be taught. You have every right as a parent to review any materials, books, homework assignments, and handouts that will be seen by your teen. After reviewing the information that will be offered to your student in most assemblies and special classes, you have the right to request that your teen opt out of such presentations.

It is impossible to stay educated with what is happening on your teen's school campus if you do not make an effort to stay involved. Volunteer with the PTA at your teen's school, and attend every meeting held by the school to which parents are invited.

Don't be afraid to call the school, visit a teacher, or schedule a meeting with a counselor or principal. Do anything and everything you can to stay involved and aware of what is happening on your teen's school campus. By taking an active role in communicating with your teen about school life, you have an opportunity to not only reinforce positive messages but also modify and correct information taught to your teen that contradicts the godly qualities you desire for him or her.

Be in Love with Your Spouse

If you are married, your teen needs to see that you love your spouse. In a world of inconsistencies, your teen will find confidence in the security and stability of your marriage. Celebrate your marriage in front of your teen, and let him or her see that your relationship with your spouse means everything to you. Take time to nurture this relationship with your spouse.

Be a Parent, Not a Pal

While I was in Montana for a speaking engagement several years ago, a girl approached me to say she had lived with her mom since her parents divorced eight years before. "But now," she said, "I'm moving in with my father in another state." She explained how difficult this move would be, considering that she was a senior in high school and that she would be leaving the friends she had grown up with.

I asked her why such a move was necessary.

She stated, "My mom lives like she is my friend. My dad lives like my dad. He lives like he loves me!"

The more I spoke with this girl, the more I could sense how insecure she felt at her mother's house. Her mother's lack of boundaries had sent the message to Angela that she could do whatever she wanted whenever she wanted with whomever she wanted. She realized the freedom her mom gave her to live as she pleased was taking her nowhere fast.

Come all the way for your teen by letting your teen see you shine in your greatest role before him or her: as a parent. Whether you are single, married, separated, or divorced, your teen needs you to be the parent in his or her life, not a pal.

Be a Voice of Love

I am amazed at the number of teens who tell me they rarely hear the words "I love you" from a parent. Of all the issues teens approach me about, this one grieves me the most.

Make it one of your life goals to go overboard in showing your teen a love that never fails. Your teen not only needs you to show it; your teen needs to daily *hear* it.

Your teen will look somewhere, to someone or something, for love, attention, support, encouragement, and security. If your teen is not finding love in the home, your teen will look elsewhere.

By working to create a clear understanding in your teen's mind that nothing your teen does will ever change your love for him or her, you will be welcoming any conversation, feeling, or anything else that is on the mind and heart of your teen. This will also let him or her know that behind every choice you make, every line you draw, every disciplinary action you enforce—behind everything—is a genuine love that will never fail.

The Beginning

As you consider what lies ahead in your family's life, hold fast to this fact: this is the beginning of a whole new journey. Satan would have you believe that the task before you is more daunting than ever and is one you are not prepared to manage. He is possibly already whispering into your ear, *You are in over your head. Just give up.*

But God has spoken to you. You know that you were created for this. And you know that the days, weeks, months, and years ahead with your teen can be the richest experience of your life.

As you begin to consider your next steps in preparing to fight like you've never fought before for your teen, slow down and enjoy the ride, because it happens only once. Wherever you are in the parenting journey, realize that this responsibility of parenting is a privilege you've been given. Every day is a new day to enjoy the beauty of the call of being a parent to one of God's beloved children.

Do you remember the first part of John 10:10 that we looked at in chapter 1? The verse read: "The thief comes only to steal and kill and destroy." Jesus reminds us that every day the battle lines are drawn and we truly are in the fight of our lives. Thankfully, Jesus didn't stop with this warning. He also provides assurance, in the second part of this verse, that He has *come all the way* for us: "I have come that they may have life, and have it to the full."

This is an appropriate verse on which to end this book, because of its remarkable promise. My hope is that, as you continue to fight the good fight and *come all the way* for your teen, both you and your teen will not only experience a God who is real and relevant for every fight you face but also daily grow in the knowledge and understanding of God's immeasurable love for you both. Go forward. Be determined. Be fearless. And live life to the full.

Praying Scripture for Your Teen

God, fill my teen with the knowledge of Your will through all spiritual wisdom and understanding. May this child live a life worthy of You and please You in every way: bearing fruit in every good work, growing in the knowledge of You, being strengthened with all power according to Your glorious might so that this child may have great endurance and patience, joyfully giving thanks to You who has qualified this child to share in the inheritance of the saints in the kingdom of light. Amen.

BASED ON COLOSSIANS 1:9–12

Acknowledgments

Thank you to everyone at WaterBrook Multnomah. David Kopp, I appreciate all you do to support our outreach to our nation's teens and their families.

To our Jeffrey Dean Ministries team, board, supporters, and prayer partners, thank you for fighting alongside me to proclaim truth to a generation of teens desperate for hope.

To all of my family, you know my love.

And to God be the glory. Though the Enemy fights to steal, kill, and destroy, I thank You, Lord, that You have already won the battle.

About the Author

A teen evangelist, counselor, and ordained pastor, Jeffrey Dean is the founder of Jeffrey Dean Ministries, serving teenagers and their families (www.jeffreydean.com, blog.jeffreydean.com). As an authority on teen culture, Jeffrey tackles everyday problems by applying solutions from the Bible. His Plugged-In Parenting seminars and *E3 Update* newsletter keep parents up to date with their teens' culture. Parents can also sign up their teens for Jeffrey's *generation Future e-news* letter or his iTunes podcast.

Jeffrey is one of the most popular public speakers in America today, speaking to and about teens. He has spoken before more than two million people at churches, conferences, camps, music festivals, prisons, military bases, and schools. He has also partnered with such ministries as Youth for Christ, Fellowship of Christian Athletes, Josh McDowell Ministry, Teen Serve Ministries, and local Boys & Girls Clubs and pregnancy resource centers across the country. He serves on the advisory board of the National Abstinence Clearinghouse.

In addition to writing *The Fight of Your Life* for parents, Jeffrey is the author of the teen books *Watch This: A Getting-There Guide to Manhood for Teen Guys, This Is Me: A Teen Girl's Guide to Becoming the Real You, One-Liner Wisdom for Today's Guys,* and *One-Liner Wisdom for Today's Girls.* He also wrote the DVD curriculum *Flood* for teenage students.

Jeffrey lives in the Nashville area with his wife, Amy, daughters Bailey and Brynnan, and canine companion Bryley.

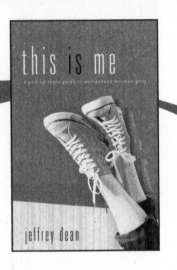